Outrageous Grace

The Gospel the Church Didn't Want You to Hear

Ron Wood

Outrageous Grace

The Gospel the Church Didn't Want You to Hear

Ron Wood

Published by Pendlebury Press Limited

20 May Road

Swinton

Manchester M27 5FR

pendleburypress@virginmedia.com

ISBN: 978-0-9935945-6-4

Imprint Pendlebury Press Limited

To Pam, who knows all this already

CONTENTS

1 INTRODUCTION

This is the story of the Secret Gospel - the **Good News that is so outrageous the church doesn't want you to hear it. It is the gospel that Jesus preached, that was so unacceptable** to the religious establishment of his time that it took him to the cross. It threatened, not the Roman state, which was big and ugly enough not to feel threatened by his beard and sandals, but the whole basis of Jewish religion. It is the gospel that today would surely put the church out of favour with all Right thinking people, and undermine the whole relationship it has with the state. It isn't putting it too strongly that it is the gospel that would put the church out of business. And yet it was there in the New Testament, spelled out by Jesus himself, enlarged upon in his parables, and proclaimed by St Paul in his letters. And it can be summed up in just four words.

So it is not new teaching. It is the original teaching of the church, which the first Christians met to celebrate with joy, but which caused them to be persecuted by a nervous empire which saw such teaching as potentially subversive and seditious. The Roman state that had not seen one man as a threat, as the Jewish leaders had, saw the movement he started as undermining its authority, so Christians died in their thousands.

Only when the Roman Empire, in its declining

years, began to see the church, popular despite persecution, as a potential ally; and the church, still raw from years of persecution, saw its espousal by Rome as the guarantee of its own survival, did that church accept a new role, and sublimate its original, wonderful gospel, and become the world's conscience. Instead of proclaiming forgiveness, free for everyone, it preached salvation as the reward for good behaviour. Instead of being the unruly party animal, gleefully blowing a squeaker, it became the frowning puritan, turning on the lights and switching off the music. The church sought approval, and became respectable.

With respectability came wealth. This little book will not be a comprehensive study of the New Testament, but it will look at parts of the Gospels, and a couple of Paul's letters. Nor can it be a history of the church, but will necessarily touch on some aspects of church history, like the Reformation, which began as a protest against some of the practices by which the church was making money- the sale of indulgences, for example. The gospel had become, not a message to be proclaimed, but a product to be sold. But there will be some cartoons.

I predict that this book will not have the effect of persuading the church to see the error of its ways, take off its badge, hang up its six-shooter, and pour itself three fingers of redeye. But I hope it will help Christians in church membership to focus better on the true Gosepel and enjoy it. And Christians who are not members of a church to see that it Doesn't Matter. Christians are like lunatics. There are more out than in.

2 FASTEN YOUR SEATBELTS

...$\mathbf{B}$ecause it's going to be a bumpy ride. We can't suddenly start going against just about everything the Church has stood for these past millennia without stirring up a bit of turbulence. We begin the only place Christian theology can begin. The Bible. And specifically, in this chapter, the Gospel of St Mark. Either Mark was the earliest Gospel, the basis for Matthew and Luke, or it's an abridged version of Matthew. Too big an argument to have here. Suffice it to say that Mark's Gospel embodies some of the earliest teaching of the church.

Bear in mind that as we consider the evidence from the Gospels, we are looking at the church's own product. The four Gospels in the New Testament were written by members of the early church, and they were accepted into the canon of scripture by the church. It wasn't the written Gospel that gave birth to the church- it was the church that gestated, wrote, edited, and finally accepted the Gospels. The church produced the Gospels to proclaim, and accepted them because they upheld the truths it was already holding as its belief. The church got to say what was scripture and what wasn't. Other gospels were written, and the decision not to include them in the canon of scripture was also made by the church. This was usually done on the grounds that these gospels were not thought to have been written by the Apostle whose name appeared on the title page- Thomas, for example. There is a Gospel of Thomas, but you won't find it in the Bible. But the real reason was that they contained material which the church regarded as heretical; that is, out of line with its own view of doctrine. So any claims by the church that its doctrines are based on the Gospels, or that the Gospels sanction anything it might choose to hold as doctrine, are a little suspect. It is far more likely the Gospels we have in our Bible were chosen because they reflected doctrines the church already held. We might criticise the Jehovah's Witnesses for rewriting the Bible to suit themselves, or for focussing only on those parts which support their doctrines, but bear in mind that the early church did something very much along the same lines. The New Testament, which forms the basis for our faith, is itself the product of the faith of those early Christians. For the first thirty years of its life, the Church had no religious writings except the Jewish, Old Testament.

Having said which, also bear in mind that the Gospel writers were men full of the Holy Spirit, and the church which compiled the canon of scripture comprised people who were also full of the Holy Spirit. So if we take that seriously, then what we have, we can trust is what God wants us to have. How we interpret it, ignore bits we don't like, or underline the bits we do, is up to us.

That was me telling you that the lifejacket is under your seat, with a whistle you can play with, and what to do if the oxygen mask drops from that little thingy over your head. Now enjoy the flight.

Why did Jesus have to die?

The starting point of the story of Jesus' suffering and death is simple enough. His enemies wanted him dead. Children in school assemblies have asked me what enemies he could have had. He was good and kind and loved everyone, right? So why did they want to have him killed? If you're only seven, these are difficult questions to answer. If you're sixty-seven, trust me, it's no easier.

What did the Jewish authorities have against Jesus? The accounts of his trial in the Gospels suggest that, far from having any real case against him that would stand up in an independent court, they were obliged to trump up charges that would convince the Roman authorities that his were capital offences. The offences Jesus is charged with don't seem to us to merit the death penalty. What comes across to us from the Gospel accounts is an establishment *unreasonably* opposed to Jesus.

In John's Gospel (18: 19-24), Jesus is questioned by Annas, the High Priest, about his disciples, and about his teaching; Jesus deflects this by reminding them that he has always spoken publicly, and there are many witnesses to what he actually said. (Some of the later gospels, known as the New Testament

Apocrypha, are based on the assertion that Jesus taught his disciples a whole lot of arcane and secret stuff. The Church rejected them largely because, as I said, they contradicted its own teachings, but also because Jesus himself declared that he taught his disciples nothing in secret, which he didn't also share with the rest of the people. Whether or not they understood it is a different matter.) Jesus tells Annas and the rest this. Which gets him a slapping. Not a metaphorical one- an actual slapping. Challenged by Jesus to say what it was in his teaching that was actually wrong, nobody answers.

The charge against Jesus brought before Pilate was that he claimed to be the King of the Jews- sedition against the current ruling regime. Whether Pilate had any idea of the Jewish expectations of a Messiah- an anointed successor to the line of King David who would free his people, we cannot tell. But, bewildered, he soon establishes that Jesus has no claim to any earthly kingdom, and tries to release him.

Blasphemy is the next charge the Jews bring against Jesus. Mark tells us that before being taken to Pontius Pilate, while Jesus was still being questioned by the priests, the specific words Jesus had used in answer to the question "Tell us if you are the Messiah, Son of God" incited the High Priest to tear his robe- the act of grief he was obliged to make on hearing blasphemy. Jesus didn't simply say, "Yes"- which would have been bad enough- he said "I Am", which is the name God gave himself to Moses, at the burning bush (Mark 14: 62, and see Exodus 3: 14). And we sense the relief of the priests that they don't need any more lying witnesses or invented charges. But to the civil authorities, they only bring out the blasphemy charge when their initial charges of sedition have been rejected.

At this point, Jesus' accusers stop using arguments and accusations altogether, and just start shouting. And eventually, Pilate gives in to pressure from the mob. The fact that he was, according to some traditions, the son-in-law of the Emperor Tiberius meant that he couldn't, as others in his position might have done, keep his head down, trying not to be noticed. The eyes of Rome were on him, and he knew it. (Actually, most of the time, the eyes of Capri were on him. Tiberius spent much of his time there, in his villa, running the Roman Empire as a sort of offshore tax dodge.) And Tiberius was a famously irritable and crusty ruler, and you wouldn't want to be on the wrong side of him. Pilate's priority was to keep order in the province, and if that was at the expense of executing one innocent man, then he was prepared to do it. The Jews actually shared this feeling. Caiaphas (John 18: 14) had said it was better for one man to die than that the nation should be crushed by the Roman response to an insurgence.

Jesus, by now, has been whipped and crowned with thorns. Pilate points to the passive, bloodied figure, and says, "Look at the man!" as if to ask how anyone could see such a pathetic, humiliated wretch as a danger. But despite his assertion that blasphemy is no crime under Roman law, the appeal that letting him live would be in itself an act of sedition against Rome sways Pilate, and Jesus is crucified.

This is gripping stuff, and the Passion story still moves us, but it doesn't really explain *why* the Jews wanted Jesus dead, to the extent that they were prepared to frame him when they had no real case against him. There were other pretenders to Messiahship, before and after Jesus, who were dealt with by the military power of Rome, because they did the proper Messiah thing, and rebelled against the occupying regime. But there is no record that their own people, let alone the religious establishment, turned against them. Amongst the ordinary Jewish people at the time, oppressed by Rome (who had famously given them nothing but sanitation, medicine, education, wine, public order, irrigation, roads, the fresh water system and public health. Oh, and peace), there was definitely a mood for a coup. What was needed was a charismatic leader. Jesus resolutely refused to be him.

It has been speculated that Jesus was seen as the Wrong Sort of Messiah, and that the very fact that he made no attempt to lead an uprising disappointed his more politically active followers, to the point of betrayal, and that a peaceful Messiah was of no use to the Jewish leadership.

In the 1960s movie *King of Kings* Judas Iscariot is a zealot- a Jewish resistance fighter, who betrays Jesus in an attempt to force his hand. "Let him feel a Roman sword at his own throat," he says, "and then he'll act." Act? This is Jeffrey Hunter! But Judas has been compared to a mother who throws her child into the deep end of the pool, expecting he will either learn to swim, or be rescued. The third alternative, that he will drown, seems not to occur to her.

The Man Who Came In Through The Roof

All the charges actually laid against Jesus, then, were either false, or not capital from the Romans' point of view. To find the real answer to the question, *Why did Jesus have to die?* we have to go further back. There is a deeper, much earlier cause of the Jews'- and especially the Pharisees'- antagonism towards him. In fact, even if he *had* been the Messiah, it would have been enough to make them reject him. The movement against Jesus began quite early. While his popularity among the ordinary people grew and grew, so did the plots against him in high places. Something Jesus said, probably often, that they heard, threatened to undermine their whole religion, and the foundations of their respectability.

The Pharisees were those who held the Law sacred. They took literally the instruction to *bind the Law around your arm, and wear it on your forehead,* by wearing phylacteries- small boxes containing scrolls of the Law. In an Israeli hospital in the 1990s, I met a woman, visiting her husband, wearing a small black box on her wrist. I asked her (in French, the only language we had in common) if it was the *Torah.*

"No," she said, flipping it open to reveal a tightly folded piece of paper, "It's my health insurance policy." The Pharisees tried diligently to keep the letter of the Law. There was a whole profession of Doctors of the Law who defined the Law finer and finer, explaining what did or did not constitute work, so the Sabbath could be kept faithfully, or what degree of behaviour with the opposite sex amounted to adultery. Jesus pulled the legs of the Pharisees because they would tithe the herbs from their little town-garden potagers as if they were farmers growing crops, while failing to observe the simple commands of love and charity. Yet the worst you could say about the Pharisees is that some of them fell into the trap of believing they really were keeping all the Law, and this became a matter of pride among them.

Now look at Mark chapter 2. Matthew and Luke also have this story, and all agree that it is early in Jesus' ministry. Jesus is in Capernaum. Mark says that he is "at home". The house is heaving with people as he teaches, including some Pharisees and teachers of the Law, who so far have found no reason to shun Jesus, or to oppose him.

Suddenly, in a shower of plaster, thatch, tiles or whatever the roof was made of, a paraplegic man on a stretcher is lowered by four friends through the hole they have just made in the roof, to land at Jesus' feet. Here is a man who cannot walk- an obvious case for healing. The whole room waits to see a miracle. And what does Jesus say?

My son, your sins are forgiven.

These words immediately cause the teachers of the Law who are present to mutter about blasphemy. Only God can forgive sins, they say, and there are proper channels! So Jesus, hearing their grumbles, demonstrates that he is able, not just to say the word, but to do the deed, and the man famously picks up his bed and walks. Jesus offers the healing as a demonstration of his power, and his power as an assurance that what he says is true.

But pity the poor Pharisee. If you have spent your whole life trying to keep the minute details of the Law, eating cold food on the Sabbath because cooking it would be work, not even picking up a pen, because that was work, too; honouring your father and mother even though they were horrible, incontinent old reprobates who called your wife a slut because she didn't iron your underpants; all this, and Jesus comes along and says to some cripple he's never even met before, *Your sins are forgiven!* Just like that. What about sacrifice, eh? What about going to the Temple, changing your everyday coin into special Temple money at an exorbitant rate of exchange, buying an animal, and not just any animal, but a perfect one, and have you noticed you can only buy the perfect ones inside the temple, and they always find fault with the one you could get for a third of the price in the market, and you take it to the priest, and he sacrifices it in the proper way, and sprinkles you with the blood and *then* says "Your sins are forgiven"? Eh? This is my whole way of life, the religion of my fathers, the very identity of my nation, everything I've held sacred, man and boy, and he just says, *Your sins are forgiven!*

It was like the time we were in Nauplion, in southern Greece. We dutifully climbed the thousand steps up to the mighty Palamede fortress, and when we got to the top, thigh muscles burning, we found everybody else had gone up the other way, by taxi.

But pause there, (we did!) and take note. Jesus has indeed said *Your sins are forgiven* to a man he has never met before. He hasn't even asked him his name, let alone enquired about the nature of his sins, and the man has offered no confession, or expression of remorse. Jesus has said nothing about repentance as a condition of forgiveness. He has asked for no promise of future good behaviour, and issued no instructions, or even suggestions, of an ethical nature. Just the simple words, *Your sins are forgiven.* This, I believe, is the turning point in the whole Gospel, and the real reason the religious establishment wanted him dead.

The rest of the chapter tells how Jesus called Levi the tax-collector as a disciple, and was criticised by the Pharisees for befriending a sinner (vv 13-17). How his attitude to fasting was criticised by the Pharisees (18-22). And how his failure to observe the Sabbath- over the trivial matter of picking and eating a few ears of wheat- rubbing the grains out was threshing, don't you know- was criticised by the

Pharisees (23-28). Before this, Jesus' ministry has been popular to the point that he was forced out of towns and into the countryside by the sheer numbers of people who would come to him. After the incident with the paraplegic man's healing, the opposition is always there, his every move being scrutinised and criticised.

Grace

The Reverend Midge Fragnetts was saved by Grace

What Jesus' enemies really couldn't buy into was *Grace*. His pronouncement that sins are forgiven, without any mention, in the case of the paraplegic, of repentance or penitence, no promise to clean up his act from then on, was as offensive to them then as it is to us now.

Jesus subsequently accepted hospitality from, and offered it to tax-collectors, who were collaborators with the Roman government, and no fit company for any respectable Jew. Some of his friends were prostitutes, to whom the same applied. He was accused of consorting with sinners, by people who never seemed to realise that they too were sinners. Had they realised they were sinners, they knew the mechanisms to go through to be forgiven, and that being forgiven required considerable effort, and even some expense, on their part. The notion of being forgiven, just on Jesus' say so, was not only unacceptable to them, but alien. Jesus wasn't even claiming to be "doing" the forgiving. He was simply stating what was the case. It's the same when I, as a priest, pronounce to the congregation in church that their sins are forgiven. I'm not forgiving them, I'm just telling them that this is the case. Your nose is running. Your flies are undone. Your sins are forgiven.

It was Jesus' saying *your sins are forgiven* and then treating everybody just as if that really was the case, that upright Pharisees found offensive.

We still, I submit, find this idea of God's grace offensive. We thirst for justice- mostly on other people. We may even be content to believe that our sins are forgiven; but what about Adolf Hitler/Pol Pot/Harold Shipman/President Assad/Insert the name of your own all-time wicked bastard? The idea that their sins are forgiven- not could be, might be, if they show the right degree of shame, contrition and repentance, but *are forgiven,* is offensive.

The Jews saw things in a more immediate sense. Caiaphas was in a difficult position. With Jewish religion and state so firmly linked historically, the loss of statehood was in itself a blow against religion. A few centuries before, Greek rulers had defiled the temple in an attempt to stamp out the Jewish religion. The great war fought by the Maccabees was followed by a period when the High Priest was also king. This ended when the Roman general Pompey invaded Judaea, and it became part of the Roman Empire. Now the Romans threatened Judaism afresh, with statues and plaques- everywhere the Emperor's image, an affront to all Jews. With their secular self-determination gone, and with numbers of their people fled and dispersed to places like Egypt, religion was all that was left to them. Their identity as a people was expressed in their faith, and their faith was played out in their religious observance. In this atmosphere, there was no scope for such radical teaching. Jesus was obviously pro-God, and pro-faith, but in the sense that his teaching undermined the whole ritual of sacrifice for atonement, he was seen to be anti-religious. Religion might be defined as what people have to do to get themselves right with

God. Jesus is saying that what we have to do is precisely nothing. If the idea caught on amongst ordinary people that God has already forgiven our sins, the Temple itself could be threatened. The national life, such as it could be under Roman rule, was centred on the Temple. Plus the equivalent of big business was based around its worship and regular sacrifice. And there was also the fear that law and order might break down. Not Roman law, but God's Law. People might carry water from the well on the Sabbath! That wasn't flippancy. If rubbing out ears of wheat between your palms was seen as threshing, then carrying water was almost heavy industry. The Jews were the people of the Law. Without the Law, who were they? Jesus was appearing to give away free what everybody else had to work for and earn. The whole basis of Jewish religion at that time was sacrifice- animal sacrifice- as atonement for sin. So Jesus was threatening to do away with religion itself. That was the real reason why he was seen as a danger to the establishment, to Judaism, and why the religious leadership wanted him silenced. And for silenced, read dead. We will see in future chapters that the church has had a history of silencing the opposition by killing people. Dan Brown didn't have to make it up. But time enough for that. We need to look at some of his parables in detail to see how Jesus spelt out his astonishing gospel, and realise for ourselves the simplicity of his message that the church itself has seen as dangerous and seditious, and has been afraid to proclaim.

3 THE LOST PARABLES OF JESUS

OK, I admit it. I only put that in to get your attention. I haven't discovered a hidden scroll. These are the parables of Jesus you already know, and they're about lost things- a sheep, a coin and a son. They comprise the whole of Luke chapter 15. They were told as a response to Jesus' legalist critics pointing out that he welcomed and ate with tax-collectors and other unspecified outcasts (who were probably prostitutes, but Luke is being a bit coy).

Repentance was never a condition of Jesus' welcome. In the story of Zacchaeus, famously up a tree in Jericho, Jesus invites himself to dinner with the diminutive tax-collector, and the *result* is his change of heart, and his promise to make reparation. But it wasn't a condition of Jesus' friendship. This idea of penitence being the result of forgiveness, rather than the precondition for it, is there in the Old Testament. In Ezekiel 36: 28-31, God says, *You will live in the land I gave your ancestors. You will be my people, and I will be your God. I will save you from everything that defiles you. I will command the corn to be plentiful, so that you will not have any more famines. I will increase the yield of your fruit trees and your fields, so there will be no more famines to disgrace you among the nations. You will remember your evil conduct and the wrongs you have committed, and you will be disgusted with yourselves because of your sins and iniquities.* God points out that he forgives his people so that they may repent. Not the other way around. Receiving all these blessings undeserved, the people will realise what heels they are.

Jesus' "lost" (sorry!) parables reflect this unconditional forgiveness in an extravagant way. Look at Luke 15: 4-7. If you have a hundred sheep, Jesus asks, and you lose one, don't you leave the ninety-nine, and go looking for it? Well, actually, since you ask, *no*. As a parable about seeking the lost, this is top-quality stuff. As a guide to keeping sheep, it leaves something to be desired. But let's play. What if the ninety-nine take advantage of the shepherd's absence, and leg it all over the prairie? Will this shepherd be worried? No. He came, he said, to seek and to save that which was lost. Sheep, he loves, but lost sheep are his real business, the grist to his mill. Finding lost sheep is, in a word, what he does. OK, three words.

But anyway, the shepherd in the story doesn't stop searching until he finds his lost sheep, and memorably carries it home on his shoulder. And there is much rejoicing. Incidentally, the image of the Good Shepherd with a sheep on board predates the Cross in Christian art. The early church, for a couple of hundred years, used it as an illustration, revelling in the thought of being found by the Lord. Only later did the Crucifixion appear, demanding a *response* from the viewer. The consciousness of Jesus' suffering and death for us cannot fail to produce feelings of guilt, remorse, and, hopefully, repentance. The Cross ousted the Good Shepherd from Christian iconography. Delight and joy were replaced by sorrow and guilt.

As a matter of interest, the sign that Constantine saw in the sky, and had painted on his legions' shields, because a voice said "In this sign, conquer", was the *chi-rho,* the superimposed Greek letters that look like P and X, another very early symbol of Christianity. The very earliest sign of a Christian was the fish, still in use on the backs of cars today. Tertullian suggested that the Cross was used very early, but nobody is really sure, and anyway it would spoil my argument.

But to our muttons! The sheep has been lost. In our children's Bibles it has wandered off, but in the original, whether its lostness was down to its own stupidity, wilfulness, or the shepherd's neglect isn't even hinted at. And despite Jesus, in verse 7, likening it to a sinner who repents, it hasn't actually made any contribution to its being found, except getting lost in the first place. It might well have bleated, and felt sorry for itself, if we used our imaginations, or read the version in our toddlers' Bible Story books. But for all Jesus tells us, it might have been quite happy where it was, munching away, lost only from the shepherd's point of view, and carried home kicking and bleating, against its will. It would have been very odd if the point of the parable was that the sheep must find its way home before the shepherd will stir himself to look for it. The point is that the sheep did nothing, but the shepherd did all that was necessary.

The second parable (Luke 15: 8-10) makes this even more clear. A lost coin can't bleat, wave, or even consciously glitter to attract attention. Its lostness is simply in the woman's perception. It cannot repent. All it can do is be found. As an enjoinder to repent and be forgiven, the parable fails. To illustrate that the act of finding and saving is entirely God's, it scores a ten.

But it is the third of these parables, (Luke 15: 11-32), the story of the Lost Son that makes the point best of all. Enough with sheep or coins already. Here is a person. By the way, I prefer the title *The Lost Son* to the older *Prodigal Son*. Prodigal just means wasteful, like the government with my tax money. The point of the story isn't what *he* did, but what his father did. Really, this is the parable of the Loving Father.

You know the story, and if you don't, I've told you where you can look it up, which might be a good idea anyway. Younger son asks his father for his share in the family fortune, cashes the cheque, runs away and spends the lot, and then hits skid row. Away from home, on his uppers, his money gone, and even envying the pigs their swill, the lad composes his little speech to his father: *Father, I have sinned against God and against you. I am no longer fit to be called your son. Treat me as one of your hired servants.* As he approaches home, his father sees him a long way off- presumably because he has been looking out, every day- and runs to him, and the son, embraced by his joyful father, doesn't get half his speech out, but it doesn't matter, because his father didn't want to hear it anyway.

The son *thought* he had to go crawling back and be penitent, or at least make the right noises to that effect. In fact, he had been forgiven from the moment he went away, and (this being in the days before mobile phones) only needed to go home to find out.

Surely these parables build up an illustration of the unconditional nature of our forgiveness, and that the initiative is with God, the shepherd, housewife and father, seeking that which can do nothing, and need do nothing to secure forgiveness.

But look! Who is this standing outside the party, refusing pointedly to go inside and join in? It is the lost son's sensible big brother, who never did anything wrong (and never had any fun, and saw his father as a boss rather than a daddy) and who speaks for us all when he says *It's not fair!* He is the one who will refuse to go to heaven if Jack the Ripper is there, who will send his own forgiveness back if he has to share it with Attila the Hun. (A couple of people sent back their MBEs when the Beatles got theirs. When Mick Jagger was knighted, I wanted to send back my Stones albums.)

The whole point of grace and forgiveness is that it isn't, by our standards, fair. God isn't fair, he's generous. Wildly, extravagantly, generous. You know cow parsley? It's four feet high. It doesn't need to be four feet high, but God says, *go on! Let's see what a weed can do!*

4 THE LETTERS TO THE ROMANS AND GALATIANS

If we're going to take seriously the concept of grace, then two of the letters of St Paul need to be considered. We're used, if we go to church regularly, to hearing them read in little chunks, and if we go to one of those churches that still uses the King James Version of the Bible, we're used to not understanding them, because sometimes Paul can go a whole page without punctuation. What we need is an overview, because Paul uses his letters to build up cogent arguments, point by point.

Paul's letter to the Romans is particularly powerful stuff, if difficult to understand. This can be explained partly by the fact that he didn't actually write it. He dictated it to a scribe named Tertius, who waves and mouths "hello Mum" at the end (16: 22). Romans has a sort of stream-of-consciousness quality about it. People suggest that Paul didn't write the letter to the Hebrews because it's different in style from his others. I think it's just as likely that Hebrews is different because Paul *did* write it. We none of us write the same as we speak.

When we were at school, it wasn't enough to give the answer to a maths problem. We had to show our Working Out. And in this letter, we have not just Paul's answer, but his working out, too, as the ideas come tumbling out, and Tertius writes it all down. Who knows, if Paul had had a word processor, he might have edited the whole thing down to half its present length. He might have tidied up some of his arguments. However, he knew where he wanted to end up, and got there eventually. Our problem with understanding Romans is that we tend to give it all the same weight- as far as we're concerned, his workings-out are just as much scripture as his conclusion. This is why the isolated bits we have read to us in church sometimes leave us more puzzled than enlightened, like watching a single episode of a TV serial without knowing who any of the characters are, or what they're talking about.

Paul hadn't yet been to Rome. He kept meaning to go, but there always seemed to be a good reason why he should be somewhere else, and besides, he couldn't get the fare together, until some Greek Christians had a whip-round. He was a tent maker by trade, and that might not have paid very well. Not a lot of call for tents in Roman cities. Fridges to Eskimos comes to mind.

What I'm going to do is have a quick scamper through the letter, giving you, fairly, I hope, the gist of Paul's arguments. This is no substitute for reading it for yourself. Don't take my word for anything. Unlike the clerics of the Middle Ages, who will disgrace a later chapter, I want you to read the Bible in your own language, and take me to task if you think my exegesis is faulty.

Near the beginning, Paul sets out his stall. *The gospel reveals how God puts people right with himself: it is through faith from beginning to end* (1: 17). And the gospel he owns can be none of those we have in the New Testament. Paul was dead before the first was written, so it must be to an earlier, oral tradition that he refers.

The rest of Chapter 1 is a tirade against the evil people who know as much as anyone can know about God, yet choose to oppose him- *their evil ways prevent the truth from being known* (1: 18). They know that God's Law says they deserve death (1: 32) but they persist.

In Chapter 2, we are told that we will be judged and rewarded for what we have done. Those who do good will be rewarded with eternal life. God's fury will descend on the wicked, with suffering and pain. Whether they do right because of the Law (the Jews) or because of their natural instincts (the Gentiles) the just will be rewarded. In fact, says Paul, the Gentiles, doing the right thing without the benefit of the Law telling them to, will become honorary Jews, by the Holy Spirit.

Chapter 3 points out that the Law can only really point up our sin. Paul quotes the Psalms, and Isaiah, to make the point that nobody is free from sin- nobody at all. We know that if God didn't love sinners, he'd only have orangutans to love. If being sinful in itself cut us off from God's love, the entire human race would be unlovable. But this is not the case. Paul says that *nobody is put right in God's sight by doing what the Law requires; what the Law does is to make man know that he has sinned* (3: 20). There is a whole chapter on this later in this book. God's way of dealing with this guilty state has nothing to do with the Law. *But by the free gift of God's grace all are put right with him through Christ Jesus, who sets them free...through their faith in him.* (3: 24-26) And then comes the killer: *We conclude that a person is put right with God only through faith, and not by doing what the Law commands* (3:28). That needs underlining. We are not put right by God by obeying the law, but by trusting him when he says that we are put right with him anyway.

You don't believe this? Look at Chapter 4. This is Paul's statement that Abraham was not righteous because he did what the Law said (How could he? He lived long before the Law was given), but because he trusted God. This is what Paul means by faith. This isn't the sort of faith implied in the Athenasian Creed- if you want to be saved, you must subscribe to these beliefs- (believing six impossible things before breakfast, like the White Queen)- but simple trust. All Jesus' exhortations to "believe in him", or "believe on him" or to "have faith in him" really do come down to this, to trust him. It isn't what we believe *about* Jesus, or whom we believe him to be that will save us, but just *trusting* him. In effect, God said to Abraham, "You are righteous- trust me on this!"

And now, trusting God when he says we have been put right with him through Jesus (really, just accepting that what he says is true), we can experience God's grace (5: 1-2). *While we were still sinners Christ died for us! By his death we are now put right with God* (5: 8). The infection of sin came into the world through Adam. His sin affects us all, and has made us sinful. But the death of Jesus reverses that. *After the one sin, came the judgement of "Guilty"; but after so many sins, comes the underserved gift of "Not guilty!"* (5: 16).

The Law was introduced in order to increase wrongdoing (5: 20). This is still true today, of course. One reason crime figures keep going up is that more and more things are made illegal. Like smoking in pubs. Hunting foxes with hounds. Putting seaweed in a telephone box. (That's true. Would I joke?) As Laurie Lee put it, in *Cider with Rosie: Crime hasn't increased, but its definition.* Anyway, says Paul, the more we sin, the more scope there is for God's grace. But he emphasises very strongly that this is no excuse to go on sinning, just to give God the exercise! (6: 1-2). This was a danger Paul saw in his own time, and what the church has been so afraid of ever since, it's reneged on proclaiming the simple gospel, and that's why this book is being written.
The church has always had, niggling away at the back of its mind the fear that if you proclaim free, unconditional forgiveness of sin, some dickheads are bound to take it as a licence to do whatever they want. Better not to take that risk. So the gospel has been constantly watered down.

The realisation of our forgiveness, Paul goes on, has given us a new life. Jesus has died to our sin. We have died to our sin. Death is the release from sin, just as it is the release from debt. Once we realise that Jesus' death is our death, and his resurrection is our resurrection, we have a clean sheet. As the old translation had it, *the wages of sin is death; but the gift of God is eternal life in Jesus Christ* (6: 23). The man with the sandwich board in Oxford Street (not the one who proclaimed that peanuts are protein, and protein equals lust- remember him?) proclaimed the first part, *The Wages of Sin is Death,* but not the second. I used to look at his other side as he went past, to see if it mentioned the Gift of God. It didn't. It said the same thing on both sides. A pity, because chapter 8 begins *There is no condemnation for those who live in union with Christ Jesus.*

God's love will never be taken from us. Nothing can come between it and us. The sentences from the end of Chapter 8 that I have read so often as a coffin follows me into church (OK, it's carried on men's shoulders) tell us that there is nothing in all creation that will ever be able to separate us from the love of God, expressed in Jesus.

Chapter 10 is great stuff. If I were being paid by the word I wouldn't hesitate to quote it all. *If you confess that Jesus is Lord and believe that God raised him from death, you will be saved, for it is by our faith that we are put right with God* (10: 9-10). And this Paul emphasises, is for everybody. Jews and Gentiles alike. (Only a Jew like St Paul would divide the whole population of the planet into Jews and gentiles. Flinders Petrie, the great archaeologist, divided it into people who were interested in ancient

Egypt, and those who weren't. But Paul is, according to his own lights, covering all the exits. Nobody gets out of salvation.) But people will only know they are saved if we tell them. And this is the reason for preaching- to share the Good News.

Chapter 12 is about serving God by serving others- living the Christian life, in joy, and above all, in forgiveness. And Chapter 13 enjoins the Christian to be a good citizen, respecting and obeying the civil authorities. But none of this makes God's love, forgiveness and salvation conditional. The love and joy and *goodness* of the Christian are the expressions of the love and forgiveness and goodness of God. *Accept one another, then...as Christ has accepted you* (15: 7).

Galatians

Did this work? Did this gospel of forgiveness and salvation through God's grace alone spread throughout a joyful church? The evidence is that it did not. Because in a later letter, written from prison in Rome to the Galatians (who lived in part of what is now Turkey, a regular hotbed of early Christianity), Paul has to correct some Christians who have been preaching what he sees as a falsehood. *I am surprised at you! In no time at all you are deserting the one who called you by the grace of Christ, and are accepting another gospel...but even if we or an angel from heaven should preach to you a gospel which is different from the one we preached to you, may he be condemned to hell!* (1: 6-9)

What is this other, different "gospel" which is being spread around? It is that in order to become a Christian, a person must first become Jewish, which, if you are of the male persuasion, makes your eyes water just thinking about it.

Paul first reiterates his credentials as an apostle, emphasising that his gospel isn't one he learned from anyone else- not even the other apostles- but from the Lord himself. We have no idea what the process of this was. But Paul insisted that he never checked with anyone else whether the Gospel he was about to preach was authentic. He just told them that he had received it from the risen Lord, and was determined to share it with as much of the world as he could. And he criticised Peter, who had had a revelation from God about the inclusion of the gentiles, but then drew back from socialising with them when he came under pressure from other Jewish Christians (2: 11-14).

We know, Paul says, *that a person is put right with God only through faith in Jesus Christ, never by doing what the Law requires* (2: 16- twice!). *I refuse to reject the grace of God. But if a person is put right with God through the Law, it means that Christ died for nothing!* (2: 21). And he repeats the example of Abraham, saying that the real chips off his old block, Jewish or otherwise, are those who do what he did- simply trust God. And if anyone gets talked into being circumcised- that is, becoming a Christian by way of fulfilling a rather painful part of the Jewish Law- then they clearly haven't grasped the good news.

If you think you have to keep this bit of the Law, you'll have to keep it all (5: 3), and that is cutting yourself off from God's grace. He uses one of his rather over-complicated similies, in which he compares the two wives of Abraham, and their children. Hagar, who was a slave, gave birth to Ishmael by the usual process of being young and fertile, and for some reason, Paul reckons she represents the covenant made between God and his people on Mount Sinai. That is, the Law. So we are slaves to the Law. But Sarah, who was a free woman, gave birth to Isaac, even though she was very old, simply because she trusted God's promise. And so we are children of Abraham, like Isaac, not Ishmael; not slaves under the Law, but free. You want to be under the Law? Fine. But you've got to be under all of it. And by trying to live by the Law means you have rejected God's grace. You want to use the edge of a penny to unscrew that? Sure you don't want to use a screwdriver? Your choice, I suppose. But I think you're being a pillock.

Paul ends his letter to the Galatians saying *Let no one give me any more trouble, because the scars I have on my body show that I am the slave of Jesus* (6: 17). I've had enough trouble, thank you, without getting this nonsense from you. We had a physics teacher at school, a Mr Landau, who had a number tattooed on his arm, from the concentration camp. We never gave him any trouble. He'd been to hell already. And St Paul hadn't been flogged, stoned, beaten up, bitten by poisonous snakes, shipwrecked and imprisoned just so he could take a lot of nonsense from a bunch of Turks who didn't know a good thing when they saw it. And his sign-off is more cursory than usual. Paul is not a happy apostle.

St Paul is at great pains to point out that we are not saved by anything we do, or don't do, but only by trusting God that what he says- *your sins are forgiven*- is true. But did this stop the church elevating the Ten Commandments to high status, and making them the centre of its ethical teaching? Not that you would notice.

5 AS WE FORGIVE THOSE?

Having established, I hope, that Jesus and St Paul both make a pretty strong case for our forgiveness depending on the grace of God and nothing but the grace of God, there is still, you might think, a problem. If there is nothing we have to do to be forgiven, is there anything we can do to forfeit our forgiveness? Are there circumstances in which God might, as it were, take it back?

First, a digression. Can we accept that Jesus' command that we love one another is based on the understanding that God and Love are such inseparable concepts that we can fairly say that God is Love? After all, that's what St John said (1 John 4: 8). And so, can we say that God's command that we forgive must also be based on the idea that God is Forgiveness? God would not command us to forgive constantly and unconditionally if he was not himself prepared to do the same.

The thing is, we might just as well forgive. We can all probably look back on times when enmity with someone made us feel bad, and reconciliation made us feel better. In fact, I would go as far as to say, *there is no point in not forgiving*. Somebody once said that forgiveness is pulling the knife out of your own wound. And God is the same. Why would he not forgive? What often prevents us from forgiving is the perception that we have that forgiveness makes us look weak. Forgiveness sends the message that we are a soft touch. Far better to retaliate. Retaliation shows that we are not to be messed with. International politics are mostly based on this concept, which doesn't help us to see a viable alternative in our personal relationships. So in this context, Jesus' message of forgiveness, turning the other cheek, giving the thief who takes your coat your shirt to go with it, is truly counter-cultural and revolutionary. And the Jews of Jesus' time, and the fledgling Church were no more ready for it than the rest of the world was. The man on the cross, inert, passive and dying, with "loser" written all over him, forgiving even those who hammered in the nails, was, in reality, not a figure the church at first wanted as a logo. So often, it replaced the naked, slumped Jesus with the robed, crowned, arms outstretched *Christus Rex*- Jesus, not dying on the cross, but reigning triumphantly from it. We once found a roadside Calvary in Brittany that showed both. Looked at one way, the cross carried a naked, dying Jesus, and St John and St Mary were looking down in sorrow. Viewed from the other side, Jesus was robed and glorified, and his mother and friend were looking up in worship. But the reality is the first version. The people who shouted to Jesus that if he came down from the cross they would believe in him probably meant it. That would have shown him to be the cool Messiah who didn't die. But Jesus didn't rise to their call. He just hung there and died. God in Jesus had no fear of appearing weak. If people mistook his loving forgiveness for weakness, he was prepared even to allow that. Not so the church. The church was reluctant to preach the simple gospel, *your sins are forgiven* because that would make it look soft. Instead, it took the stance of being tough on sin, tough on the causes of sin.

Meanwhile, back at the plot, the Lord's Prayer, which we say every day and twice on Sundays, famously contains the line ...*and forgive us our sins, as we forgive those who sin against us*. Notice I said sins, and not trespasses, to show how up-to-date and right on I am? This sounds like we are asking God to make our forgiveness conditional. Only forgive us our sins, to the same degree we forgive other people theirs. There is the implication that if we are not forgiving people, we cannot expect God to forgive us. Are we here recognising that the gospel is, after all, too good to be true (as we always suspected), so we point out to God that we agree with him that he is being over-generous, so could he perhaps limit his forgiveness to match our own?

Rather than accept that we are made in the image of God, we prefer to make God in our image. Just as the gods of the Greeks were perceived as nothing more really than big people, who loved, and fought, cheated and connived, so we tend to think of God in human terms. This was, in fact, why God became human in Jesus, so we know, in our terms, what he is like; but it would be a mistake to take our human characteristics, and assume that they are therefore God's, only on a larger scale. Because we find forgiveness difficult, we might think that God, too, has the same problem. So that clause in the

Lord's prayer? I think it may be a case of saying to God, *forgive us our sins, because look! We forgive other people!* Not *if* we forgive others- we do, because we're Christians, and want to be like Jesus.

Matthew places the Lord's Prayer early in Jesus' ministry, in chapter 6, as part of the great Sermon on the Mount. Luke has it later, but both agree it was the response to Jesus' followers asking him for teaching about prayer. Rabbis taught their disciples to pray effectively. John the Baptist did, too. Was Jesus going to be an exception? No, but it seems he complied with their request with a little reluctance, and gave as little teaching as he thought he could get away with. But even this brief, stripped-down-to-the-bare-essentials prayer contains the request for forgiveness, and the promise of forgivingness.

This is, of course, before the death of Jesus. Our sins are forgiven through his crucifixion. So are the sins of all those between his time and ours. And those who lived and died before him, right back to the time humanity first acquired a conscience. But at what point in his ministry did Jesus understand this? Could there have been a time when his own appreciation of the mechanism of forgiveness was incomplete? To assume so would make some of our problem go away, but it would hardly be fair to the text of the Gospels. And even if I am in favour of the church letting go of some of its own, non-Biblical teachings and dubious traditions, the Lord's Prayer is non-negotiable.

William Barclay, who produced *The Daily Study*

Bible (and who did, unwittingly, write a whole lot of my early sermons), in his commentary on John 20: 23, refers to Jesus' words, *If you remit the sins of anyone, they are remitted; if you retain them, they are retained.* And then, by way of commentary, he says, *One thing is certain- no man can forgive any other man's sins.* And I bristle a bit.

True, I suppose, that nobody can forgive any other's sins *against God,* but we can certainly forgive those who sin against us, which is what the Lord's Prayer is about. Barclay admits that *it is the great privilege of the church to convey the message of God's forgiveness to men.* We can't forgive other's sins against God, because he has done so already. Which brings me back to my question, whether there are circumstances in which God might rescind our forgiveness, and overwrite on our absolution, *stet*?

Luke 18: 21-35 contains the parable of the unforgiving servant. Read it. Now. Go on. Peter asks Jesus how often he is expected to forgive someone before he is allowed to thump him. His question is, in effect, whether there is a limit on the expectation of his own forgiving-ness. He thinks he is being more than reasonable. *If my brother keeps on sinning against me,* (Does he mean that literally? Is he talking about Andrew?) *how many times do I have to forgive him? Seven times?*

No, says Jesus, *seventy times seven times.* And you know he doesn't mean four hundred and ninety.

Because, Jesus goes on, *the Kingdom of heaven is like this…*and he tells the story of a servant who owes his

king "millions of pounds" according to the Good
News Bible, or ten thousand talents in the older
versions. I used to think this was an improbable
figure plucked out of the air for its total ridicability,
until a French bank clerk, in 2008, lost his bank three
and a half thousand million pounds. That's *three and a
half thousand million pounds!* Imagine if he had gone to
his boss, and said, *etez patient avec moi, et je will pay
vous tout!* They would have laughed. *Oh oui? Tu es
planning to live sept cent ans? Tirez l'autre jamb!*

The king in the parable thinks this is pretty
funny, too. Instead of selling the servant and his
family into slavery, he simply forgives the whole
debt. A king is prepared to write off millions,
because he knows his servant is never going to be
able to pay him back anyway. Up till now, the
perfect parable of forgiveness. God forgives us
because he might as well. We haven't a hope of
paying him back. All the talk about paying back is
bullshit. The servant knows it. The king knows it. He
forgives because he has nothing to lose, and because
forgiving makes him feel good, whereas selling a man
and his family into slavery would leave a bad taste in
his mouth and spoil his banquet. Nothing like
screams from the dungeon to put you off your cutlet.

But then, our servant, with, we assume, a
weight off his shoulders and a spring in his step, goes
off, and bumps into a fellow-servant who owes him
the price of a pint. Fellow-servant, with our hero's
hands unexpectedly around his throat, says, *be patient
with me, and I will pay you back,* and from him, it's a

perfectly reasonable proposition. We're not talking the National Debt here, just a few quid. But the forgiven servant is having none of it, and really does have his fellow-servant thrown into prison. (Debtor's prison has always puzzled me. A man in prison can do nothing to raise funds to pay off his debt, except appeal to friends or money-lenders, which only shifts the problem. But I digress. Again.)

The king, hearing of this unforgiving behaviour waxes wrathful, tears him off a strip, and throws him into prison until he pays back the whole debt. What he had owed him in the first place, before he forgave him. In other words, his former forgiveness is retracted. He had not thrown away the paperwork, or buried in the depths of the sea, as Isaiah put it. He had merely filed it away, and for his unforgiveness, the servant is now unforgiven once more. *And that,* Jesus tells Peter, *is how my Father will treat you, if you don't forgive one another from your heart.*

Which blows my whole theory, the whole concept of this book, of unconditional, unmerited forgiveness, clear out of the water, doesn't it? If we take the parable at face value, and take the Lord's Prayer into consideration, forgiveness is conditional on our forgiving others.

Suppose you just trust me for a minute, while I reiterate my position, that our sins are forgiven, no ifs, buts or maybes. And God is *not* going to retract that forgiveness, ever. This is my secret Gospel, the bee in my bonnet.

But if I am not a forgiving person, how can I

appreciate my own forgiveness? If I only want a God I have made in my own image, isn't he going to be, like me, mean-spirited and grudging? And bearing grudges, too. When I have a quarrel with you, I rake up every quarrel we've ever had, and remind you once again of all the ways you always irritate me. So how can I expect God to be any different?

So only a forgiving person can really take on board the notion of his own forgiveness. And if you do not think you are forgiven, you might as well not be. If I deposit a thousand pounds in your bank account and don't tell you, it does you no good. Actually, make that a million. If I'm talking imaginary money, then like Han Solo, I can imagine quite a lot. And if I tell you I've done it, and you don't believe me, it still does you no good. Fine. If you don't want my money, I can't make you take it. We can ignore God's forgiveness, and live in the prison of our guilt.

This should be the church's mission- to proclaim forgiveness and freedom, and to encourage the sharing of forgiveness- like passing on the joke you just heard.

6 CHURCH AND STATE: THE EARLY YEARS

Here we take a break from theology for a while, and do some history instead. R.E., I remember, was with Mr King, who was kind and avuncular, and made us draw maps of the journeys of St Paul because he had to, but told us of God's love because it was too good not to share. History was with Mr "Daddy" Davies, who was irascible and grumpy, blamed everything on America, and America on George III. Yet somehow I learned some history. So take that gum out of your mouth and pay attention.

The relationships between states and religions have not always been friendly. No state ever seems to have realised that persecution doesn't make a religion go away, it just stiffens its resolve to survive. So Christianity grew stronger under persecution by the Roman state, which saw it as subversive, for reasons I will explain in a minute (unless you are a very slow reader, in which case it will be nearer five). Christians were, and still are, persecuted by Communist states, where they flourish in secret, and the practice of Christianity is outlawed in some Islamic states, where statistics are much harder to come by. But more often, religion and state get along on more or less friendly terms. Maybe each respects the other's points of view, maybe there is no real conflict of interest. In some Islamic countries, Sharia law prevails- the state law is the religious law, so there is no conflict between the two. My brother-in-law once tried to eat a choc-ice in the Gulf States during Ramadan. His protests that he was a Christian only seemed to make it worse. When he asked the petrol station owner who was slapping it out of his hand why he had sold it to him in the first place, there was no coherent answer. The government of Burma came down heavily on protests led by Buddhist monks. What it comes down to is whether the state sees religion as a threat to law and order, or its ally in keeping it.

To go back to the first example. Once Roman Emperors decided they were divine- Caligula appears to have been the first to claim divinity during his own lifetime- the state of Rome was, effectively, God's kingdom on earth. The head of state was a god. A Roman was obliged to worship the Emperor to demonstrate his allegiance to the state. The person of the Emperor embodied the state. This Emperor-worship usually consisted, in practice, of offering a token pinch of incense, which was provided, on a brazier set up for the purpose in front of a bust or statue of the Emperor. It was a symbolic act, not even of lip service, as one wasn't even required to say anything. In a largely polytheistic state, this was generally acceptable.

Sprinkle Sprinkle

But for a Christian (or a Jew, for that matter) to be seen to offer worship to any other god but God- the God who revealed himself in Jesus, was *anathema*, from the Greek word for accursed. There were Christians who would make a point of hissing loudly as they passed any pagan temple, so to make even this tiny, symbolic act was abhorrent, and many died martyrs' deaths rather than do it. They may well have been faithful, patriotic Romans, serving in its armies, working in its civil service, with no thought at all of treason or sedition. They would obey the Emperor's laws and edicts, and pay him all honour and taxes due to an earthly ruler. They just wouldn't acknowledge him as a god. Some Christians would explain pedantically, as they paid their taxes, that they were not doing this because the Emperor demanded it, but because *their* Lord commanded it- render unto Caesar the things that are Caesar's and all that.

The opponents of the church accused Christians of all sorts of dark deeds, in order to justify persecuting them. Incest (all that talk about loving your brothers and sisters), cannibalism (a wilful misunderstanding of the sharing of bread and wine, as the Body and Blood of Christ), group sex (the communal meal was known as an *agape,* or love feast- nudge nudge, know what I mean?). As a counter to this, Christians were enjoined by their leaders all the more to uphold the highest of moral standards- not simply to be good, but to be seen to be good. Those who were caught with their hands in the till, or up their mistresses' skirts, were expelled from the fellowship- just as our politicians today can expect to lose their jobs, not for lapses of morality *per se*, but if those lapses embarrass the party.

And then the church began to see itself as the vessel of salvation. Peter, before the Jewish council, had said, *Salvation is to be found through him [Jesus] alone; in all the world there is no one else whom God has given who can save us* (Acts 4: 12). But it wasn't long before the church began to see itself as the agent of God's salvation, and then the sole agent. And once the church had claimed salvation as its exclusive, those cast from it were necessarily excluded from salvation. Suddenly, the church was no place for a sinner. And salvation was a matter, not of being forgiven by God, but of being forgiven and re-admitted to the church.

But this was internal politics, of no more interest to the authorities than Jesus' so-called blasphemies had been to Pontius Pilate. Christians came to be judged in the eyes of Rome, not on their morality, their love, their kindness, service or acts of charity, but on their willingness to partake in this notion of the state, the state being Rome; and persecuted to the point of martyrdom for their failure.

Was it something I said?

The church was sometimes forced into an ambivalent attitude. In times of active persecution, Christians would sometimes greet each other with a cheerful "May you gain your crown." Martyrdom was seen as an honour. Ignatius of Antioch, in his letter to the Ephesians in 104, written as he journeyed to Rome as a prisoner, claimed to be looking forward to his encounter with the wild beasts in the arena. But a martyr's goods were confiscated by the state. And here was a problem. The church in the Acts of the Apostles pooled its resources. People shared everything they had. Ananias and his wife, Sapphira, were famously struck dead for lying about this. But even after this experiment in Christian communism was abandoned (it seems that the delay in Jesus' second coming, and the realisation that normal life had to go on was the main reason for this), a wealthy Christian might well be bankrolling his church, in the sense of contributing to its charitable works. The church organisation itself, in those days, was very cheap to run. So the dilemma, between wishing him the crown of martyrdom, and needing his money, was sometimes acute. There were cases of Christians being encouraged to recant their faith and save their lives by sprinkling the incense, with the promise of forgiveness afterwards. Even in those early days, the church was prepared to sacrifice its principles for financial reasons.

But the young Church's fortunes were about to change forever. The Emperor Constantine ruled from 306 to 338 over a declining empire. Faith in its gods was becoming nominal, and Emperors, often short-lived, failed to live up to any standards of divinity. Constantine the Great, (a Yorkshireman. Not a lot of people know that!) saw Christianity as a potentially powerful unifying force. He adopted Christianity as the religion of the state. Christians, delighted to be free at last from persecution, took to their new role with enthusiasm. The Church went from being persecuted, to being tolerated. Then from being one of the religions of the Empire, to being the one, official religion. In this atmosphere, to preach free, unconditional forgiveness of sin, through God's grace only, would have been difficult, to say the least. There was the danger, which Paul had met, and countered, that Christians would trade on this forgiveness, and the church would be seen as morally lax, all but encouraging sinners. And what state, particularly a failing empire, barely able to impose law and order within its borders, let alone defend itself from barbarian outsiders, wanted to embrace a faith that appeared to make light of sin? For the pronouncement that sin was forgiven without reserve was bound, in some quarters, to be seen as condoning sin. And condoning sin was tantamount to condoning crime, as the two were often seen to be the same. The Empire could not tolerate a church that told thieves, or even murderers, that their sins were forgiven by a merciful God. What it wanted was a church that would preach an all-seeing God, a God of justice, who would punish evildoers, even if they slipped through the hands of the earthly law enforcers. Where the police failed, God was there as backstop.

Perhaps this is inevitable once Church and State interact like this. It is the State's job to impose law and order, to detect, try and punish (or even attempt to reform!) the criminal. It should be the church's joy (not a typo- I do mean joy) to proclaim God's mercy on all sinners, even criminals. It can proclaim God's forgiveness even to the convict in his cell, although the man on the chain-gang might find it hard to actually *feel* forgiven. But the church acted like the woman who married the golf addict, and besotted with the man, became his faithful caddie.

So the die was cast. The Christian church had stopped being a joyful club of forgiven sinners, and became a society of good, moral citizens. Instead of accepting its own forgiveness, and forgiving others in return, it had become censorious, casting out the sinner from its midst, to keep its respectable image intact. From now on, the church was going to be seen very much in moral terms, setting an example, and worse still, being a religion.

The Christianity that Constantine adopted wasn't at that time, any more than it is now, a homogenous body of people all believing the same things. There were discussions, which as often as not developed into disputes, about such matters as how or whether Jesus could be both totally human and truly divine. About how God himself could be Father, Son and Holy Spirit and still be just the One

God. Constantine called everyone together at Nicea in 325, to try and sort it all out. The Christians from Alexandria were represented, not by their bishop Alexander, but by his protégé, Athenasius. They had enough clout to vote down the teachings of Arius, who denied that the Word of God was co-eternal with God the Father, and that Jesus was fully divine. (It didn't go away- Jehovah's Witnesses might not know it, but they are Arians). Athenasius devoted a lot of his subsequent career as the next Bishop of Alexandria to opposing the Arians. The Council of Nicea gave us the Nicene Creed, which is phrased the way it is to counter what the church- the influential majority of it, that is- considered heresies. For example, it begins *I believe in one God* as opposed to three. Athenasius expanded that creed into the four pages of impeccable stuff you'll find in the Book of Common Prayer just after Evensong. The church was defining itself, to the exclusion of others, by what it believed. I would remind members of the Prayer Book Society that the Book prescribes the Athenasian Creed to be recited at Christmas, Epiphany, Easter, Pentecost, and a whole bunch of saints' days. You don't have to make up an excuse- come Easter, you go right ahead.

The Athenasian Creed begins: *Whosoever will be saved, before all things it is necessary that he hold the Catholic faith. Which faith except every one do keep whole and undefiled, without doubt he shall perish everlastingly.*

Salvation, in other words, depends on subscribing to a whole list of doctrines, defining precisely the relationship between the Persons of the Holy Trinity. The Creed concludes:

And they that have done good shall go into life everlasting, and they that have done evil into everlasting fire. This is the Catholic faith: which except a man believe faithfully, he cannot be saved.

Not a word about forgiveness of sin at all. The good- that is, members of the church, as defined by these doctrines, get to go to heaven; the wicked- those who hold other beliefs, go to hell, and the church gets to say which is which. So as soon as it became the Official Church of the Roman Empire (is that like being the Official Salted Snack of the Rugby World Cup?) the church sought to exclude not only those who failed its rigorous tests of morality, but also those who couldn't subscribe to its defined list of doctrines- doctrines which, it has to be said, are not universally accepted, or even understood, by Christians today. And in doing so, it excluded those outside the church from salvation. True, it was still, in a way, upholding Paul's great tenet that we are saved by faith. But that word- faith- had changed meaning. Instead of meaning simple trust in God and his grace, faith was now a rigidly defined list of things it was necessary to believe. Failure to believe was called heresy. Heretics were outside the church. The church had claimed the exclusive rights to salvation. *Your sins are forgiven* had been quietly hidden away.

7 THE MORMON EXAMPLE

So far, I have been trying to make the case that the early church went back on what should have been its guiding principles- which should really have stopped it being an organisation at all, let alone an organised religion- because it wanted the approval of the state. It wanted the protection and prestige that being, not just a religion, but the official state religion brought with it. I guess some readers, if I still have any, will be questioning whether any religion would compromise its ideals for the sake of state approval. Surely the history of Christianity is of state persecution, and uncompromising individuals suffering martyrdom rather than recant their faith? And yet there are examples, as I have said, of the church being unwilling to lose its wealthy members, and their money, and so it gave them the special dispensation not to die the martyr's death, but to live, and continue to support the church.

But would a whole church sacrifice its founding tenet, merely to win the approval of a secular authority? If you still doubt, I present...*the Mormons*. The Church of Jesus Christ of Latter-day Saints.

The founder of the Mormon Church, Joseph Smith, received a divine revelation in 1843 that polygamy (the Mormons called it "plural marriage") was not only allowed, but to be encouraged. *Doctrines and Covenants* published in 1876, and second only to *The Book of Mormon* in importance, included plural marriage as a doctrine, and it became one of the hallmarks of the church, and a bone of contention to those outside it, who saw it as nothing more than the approval of adultery.

Smith and the church hierarchy practiced it, although, aware that it could leave them open to the charge of immorality, Smith always denied that he had more than one wife. But Joseph Smith lived his whole life within the jurisdiction of the United States, where polygamy was illegal. It was largely their wish to continue the practice of plural marriage that led the Mormons to move west, under Smith's successor, Brigham Young, away from United States territory, and establish themselves in Utah, where they founded Salt Lake City.

In 1862, Abraham Lincoln signed what was known as the Morrill Anti-bigamy Act, with the intention of outlawing any Mormons still under United States jurisdiction. But the frontier was moving west, too, and the United States caught up with the Mormons. They found themselves surrounded by the growing Union. But Brigham Young declared in 1866, *If Utah will not be admitted to the Union until it abandons polygamy, we shall never be admitted*. In 1871, he was indicted for adultery.

In 1882, George Q Cannon, a Mormon, was denied his seat in the House of Representatives for polygamy. In 1890, the church Manifesto, despite protests from some traditionalists, banned the practice of plural marriage, and in 1896, Utah became the 45th State of the Union.

In today's United States, adultery is no longer a criminal offence, although bigamy still is, of course. But there is a breakaway, traditionalist group of Mormons who have returned to polygamy- only the first marriage being recognised in federal law- because now they can. But the main body of the Mormon Church abandoned its divinely revealed doctrine in return for political acceptance, echoing what the Christian Church had done fifteen hundred years earlier.

I quote this- and all the information is from websites set up by the Church of Jesus Christ of Latter-day Saints- to illustrate the point that if push comes to shove, if a church is faced with a choice between holding to a doctrine that will cause it to be viewed with suspicion, vilified, persecuted and martyred, and surviving, it will choose to survive. The church in the Roman Empire did, and the church in the world today does. The world sees Christians as odd enough as it is. If it really grasped the gospel- the one we are afraid to preach, it would think us odder yet.

Outlaws 2   Inlaws 127

8 JOINING THE CLUB

Back in the Old Testament, Israel was truly God's people. The original covenant between them was spelled out by God himself. *You will be my people, and I will be your God.* There was no law other than God's Law, and in times of conflict, when the Israelites were threatened by the Midianites, Jebusites, Anthracites or Marmites, a charismatic leader could be relied on to appear and rally the militia to see off the invader. That word *charismatic* is deliberate. It means gifted, and the leaders- the Judges, as the Bible calls them- were chosen by God, given the confidence and strength they needed by God, advised and instructed by God, and generally gave God the credit for the victory. Gideon, one of these leaders, was approached after the war with the Midianites, and asked to be the people's king, but he refused. In peacetime, it was the prophet, speaking and interpreting God's word, who was a sort of leader, in as much as there was one at all. The last of these was Samuel. But as Samuel the prophet grew old, and his sons seemed venal, and inadequate to succeed him, the people sent delegates to him, saying *Appoint a king to rule over us, so that we will have a king as other countries have* (I Samuel 8: 5).

The urge to be like "the other countries" was strong. Samuel argued with them. He told them what a monarchy would mean- oppression, taxation, all the machinery of the State, a drain on the people's energy and money. But the people persisted. *No! We want a king, so that we can be like other nations!*

Just as Israel was never meant to be like "the other nations," the Church ought to be more aware that Christianity is not a religion. It was never meant to be a religion. It is the antidote to religion. Religion is whatever people feel they have to do to get right with whatever god they have. Religion is the result of the recognition that mankind is dependent on its gods for the blessings of the natural world, or that the relationship between mankind and its gods is soured by man's sin. Religion is about mankind doing what he has to do to please the gods, or heal the breach. Sacrifice and penance to remove sin. Sacrificing virgins (or prisoners of war if virgins are a bit thin on the ground), to ensure the sun doesn't go away altogether in midwinter, and we defeat our enemies. Religion specifies what people have to do, in terms of ritual, or say in prayer, to get right with their god or gods.

Christianity ought to be proclaiming the end to all that. We need do nothing to please God, because he loves us to bits anyway. He is totally besotted by us. His love is totally unconditional, and nothing will ever be able to separate us from it. We need do nothing to secure forgiveness, because we are forgiven already, completely and absolutely. Not only is there nothing we can do, but there is nothing we have to do, to secure God's love and forgiveness.

But in practice, the church, almost from its

beginning, has been more like ancient Israel. When the Roman Empire at first made Christianity legal, it became one religion amongst the many. It didn't then raise so much as a timid hand to claim that actually, sir, if you please, we're not a religion. When it became the Official Religion of the Roman Empire, it caved in altogether, and accepted the position, the badge, and the prestige.

We want to be like other religions. We can't, apparently, just be a loose conglomeration of people rejoicing in our forgiveness, and spreading that good news around, and telling other sinners like us that their sins are forgiven, just like ours. We need to define ourselves, so we know who is in, and who isn't. We want to be a club, and what's worse, we want to be an Organisation. We want rituals like other religions! Initiation ceremonies, and processions! Leaders, and hierarchy. Some spiffy buildings- not just the local community hall, hired for the morning. But first, above all, we want a code of ethics like other religions. Some religions are based around their ethical principles. Others attach their moral code to their basic faith. But wait- what is this we find in the Old Testament? It is the Ten Commandments. Carved on slabs of stone by the finger of God himself. Made to last. Look at that craftsmanship. And so we take the Ten Commandments, and instead of drawing glasses and a moustache on them saying *Look what God has forgiven us from!* we make them our prescriptive code of behaviour, our standard of goodness. So the Ten

Commandments will have a whole chapter to themselves, not to mention a very long, if slightly camp movie with Charlton Heston as Moses.

9 REASONS TO FEEL GUILTY, PARTS ONE TO TEN

The Ten Commandments are found at the beginning of Exodus chapter 20, and also in Deuteronomy 5. They are also, for the benefit of the long-sighted, often found written up in big letters on the walls of English parish churches. In one small Dorset church (Gussage St Andrew, since you ask), two large black boards dominate a whole wall, with the Commandments written in faded gold. At the bottom, the boards appear to be signed, BENJAMIN BILES, CHURCHWARDEN, by far the largest lettering on them. Gussage St Andrew had no squire, magistrate or even village policeman. So Mr Biles, as a Victorian churchwarden, was a pillar of his community, and in the interests of law and order, he was more than happy to put his name to God's law- or to invoke God's law in his desire for a peaceful and well-ordered society, which Gussage St Andrew has always been, except for a bit of smuggling, and a murder in 1905, and Wendy's handbag being stolen from her car.

The Commandments begin with the statement *I am the Lord your God who brought you out of Egypt where you were slaves.* Clearly, then, they are aimed at the Jewish people, but despite this, I have met people whose main claim to being a Christian is that they try to live their lives according to the Ten Commandments. (I like that "try"!)

The fact that they were originally given to a nomadic people camping somewhere between Egypt and the Promised Land has never stopped anybody from assuming they are for all people, for all time. And the patent impossibility of living up to them didn't, for very long, stop the church from holding them up as its own ethical code, despite the teachings of St Paul that all they have ever been is a definition of sin. But more of that later.

Worship no god but me. God asks his people to define themselves by their worship of him. He is their identity. The ancient Egyptians used hieroglyphs called determinatives at the end of some words, to make the meaning plainer. When they came to name foreign peoples, the god those people worshipped might be drawn at the end to highlight who they were. But the Habiru- the Hebrews- were a problem, because their God had no image. They knew that the God of the Habiru was worshipped on hills and high places, so the hieroglyph that we still use to denote uneven road surfaces, the one that looks like one of Katie Price's discarded bras, was tacked on the end. God was a hill-god, and he defined who the Habiru were. This commandment is saying, lose sight of God, and you lose your identity. Samuel the prophet knew this, and said so, trying to resist the call of the Israelites for a king, so they could be like other nations (I Samuel 8: 4-8). Samuel knew that what they were really doing was rejecting the idea of identifying themselves as the people of God.

Do not make for yourselves images of anything in heaven or on earth or in the water under the earth. Do not bow down to any idol or worship it. Bart Simpson is shown at the beginning of each episode of *The Simpsons* writing lines on the blackboard. One of my favourites is "I will not carve gods." Apart from Bart, few of us are really tempted to make unto ourselves any idol. Having said which, a Martian might well be excused for thinking that the Orthodox churches, venerating icons, kissing them and bowing before them, or the Roman Catholic church, with its statues, altarpieces and relics, or even our simple parish churches with a figure of the dying Jesus on their altar crosses, are all in breach of this commandment. We excuse ourselves by saying we don't worship the image, but the God it represents, but our Hindu friends say the same thing. Some of the old mosques, and most modern ones, have no representational art in them at all. Some of the very oldest ones have mosaic or painted scenes of landscapes full of animals, birds and vegetation, but generally, Muslims are better at keeping this particular commandment than we are.

If having a church full of images really helps us to concentrate our thoughts on God, and worship him better, then I can't say it's wrong. But what poor people we are! We might say a crucifix is nothing but an *aide memoire,* but most of us would be horrified at the thought of a crucifix being trampled or abused. We might say the statue of Our Lady is just a statue, but aren't there a lot of stories of miracles performed by just a statue?

The intention of the commandment is clearly that nothing, especially nothing man-made, be raised to the status of a god. Nothing is to detract from the worship we offer God. Nothing in our lives is more important than God. The church has often interpreted this to mean that nothing is more important than going to church. An extra commandment has been inserted. *Thou shalt not skip church.* Your girlfriend is a nurse, and Sunday morning is the only chance you have to see her? That was no excuse at the church I attended in the sixties. Nothing was more important than God, and this was made manifest in Nothing is More Important than Going to Church.

Do not use my name for evil purposes. "Oh my God!" has become the universal expression, usually accompanied by covering the face with both hands, by which teenage girls express delight, horror, surprise, or just about anything, really. Most bad language is either religious or sexual in origin, but Christians still find the use of God's, or Jesus' name offensive. But you could also say this commandment is better expressed in older translations. *Thou shalt not take the name of the Lord thy God in vain.* In other words, calling yourself a Christian- *ie* taking the name of your God, and then acting like a total ratbag, gives God a bad name. And it makes him angry. That's his reputation we're besmirching. People looking for a stick to beat the church with find the crusades a suitably stout one. All sorts of cruelty, by crusader knights with crosses on their surcoats. Atrocities done in the name of Jesus Christ. And yet here I am, never using God's name as an expletive, or raising my crossbow to a Saracen, but failing in all sorts of ways to live up to the name of Christ, even when I'm wearing my dog collar. Guilty.

Keep the Sabbath holy. Holy means *different.* If you have to work six days a week, you need a day off. The early revolutionary government in Russia tried a seven day week, and it failed. Christians, very early on, to commemorate the Resurrection, kept the first day of the week as their day of rest and worship, rather than the seventh, the Jewish Sabbath. Islam keeps Friday as its holy day. My son, who is a paediatric intensive-care nurse, keeps whatever day off he can get. My grandmother told me stories of her childhood, of Sundays made miserable by no toys, no books that weren't actually religious, best clothes, no outdoor play...I'm surprised her faith survived it. The old lady in *Whisky Galore* who locks her adult son in his room rather than have him violate the Sabbath is a great comic creation, but she's no caricature.

But this is, believe it or not, a commandment to have Fun. All work and no play, as they say. The Sabbath, whenever you can get it, is for rest and recreation. And notice there is *nothing in the commandment about going to church.* That was never a commandment, only an option. Never a duty, only a delight. But we came to interpret *holy* as *religious,* and so a lot of hardworking people never had any real leisure time at all. Instead of just keeping the day different, by not doing any work, the church taught us to keep Sunday religious, and that meant going to church. I still meet old people who were forced to go to church three times on a Sunday, and so as soon as they were out of their parents' influence, they stopped going at all, with a huge sigh of relief. Even in the Old Testament, worship on the Sabbath was because it was the day people were free from work. They weren't free from work solely so they could worship.

Respect your father and your mother, so that you may live a long time in the land that I am giving you. It's sad that this had to be written into the code of Law at all, but respect for parents isn't actually part of our natural way of being. Jesus had heard of cases where people had used the small print of the law to avoid caring for their parents (Mark 7: 9-13), which had been upheld by the legal experts. This is the only commandment that God justifies with a *because.* Family life, based on respect for parents, is the basis for a strong society, and if the race is to last in its homeland (this has nothing to do with individual longevity), then respect for parents is a priority. The commandments were designed to keep Israel together as a healthy, sane, recognisable entity. But Benjamin Biles, if his children gave him any lip, could always point to number five and say, "See?"

Do not commit murder. It ought to be obvious that this commandment enshrines the concept that human life is sacred. Murder has always been seen as the worst of crimes in most societies, and if it wasn't one of the Ten Commandments, we'd wonder why on earth not. Older translations had *Thou shalt not kill*, and placards bearing this form of words were carried outside prisons as the debate over capital punishment became more heated- for example, when Ruth Ellis became the last woman to be executed in Britain. But there was usually a distinction being made between state and individual. The state found *Do not commit murder* the most acceptable rendition, as well as the most accurate, because it could then excuse killing people in war, executing criminals, or legalising abortion, on the grounds that it isn't murder. Murder became what the state said it was. Capital punishment wasn't murder because we said it wasn't. We executed murderers to show how seriously we took the commandment not to kill.

Do not commit adultery. When I was thirteen, with the rest of my confirmation group, Father Wright, our elderly vicar, reeking of pipe-tobacco, went through the commandments just like I am now.

When he got to this one, there we all were, full of pubescent expectation. He had got to the good bit at last. And filling his pipe, tamping down the tobacco with a brown and practiced thumb, he said, *Milkmen used to sometimes pass off skimmed milk as whole milk by adding yellow colour to it, to make it look creamy. This was called adulteration. There are laws against it now.* And that was all he said, I promise. He went straight on to *thou shalt not steal.*

Before the days of contraception, when sex was pretty well bound to end in pregnancy, the idea of sex for pure recreation was a very odd one. I mean, if you didn't want to have a baby, or already knew you couldn't have a baby, why bother with it at all?

There was a time when sex was what defined marriage. Notice the commandment says nothing about sex before marriage. In ancient Israel, there was no such thing. This is because if a couple started sleeping together, with or without telling other people and having a party, that implied a commitment to each other, which was called marriage. Any subsequent sex outside that initial union was considered adultery. St Paul believed this. He says that if a man's first sexual encounter is with a prostitute, then they're married (I Corinthians 6: 16), which seems rather an extreme view to us. The reasoning was that a man was entitled to know that any child he was bringing up was actually his. This is why it was always (and in Islamic law still is) a much more serious offence for a married woman to have sex with another man, than for a married man to have sex with another woman. What was being judged wasn't just the behaviour, but the result- pregnancy, and the birth of a child. But behind the commandment is the principle that because of the bond between two people it creates and constitutes, sex is never to be undertaken lightly. And that sex outside a relationship once established, is a betrayal of trust.

It was only in the Middle Ages that the church started saying that unless a couple had been married *in church*, according to its rites and ceremonies, with a priest there to do the honours, they weren't married at all. And it started referring to loving, faithful couples, committed exclusively to each other for life, as Living In Sin. And the church has come pretty near to teaching that sex itself is something nasty- necessary for procreation, but really to be avoided otherwise. For a man to want sex was called Lust. For a woman to want sex was almost unthinkable. Ugh. Move on.

Do not steal. Paper clips, biros, wages that you are given that you didn't actually earn because you were having a sickie. The insurance money because they can afford it. Time. There are all sorts of ways of stealing that have nothing to do with wearing an unconvincing mask and carrying a bag with *swag* written on it. Most societies in history have regarded property as important, and its theft as dishonesty. The first Europeans to land on Easter Island in the eighteenth century had their hats taken from their heads by the local people who had no concept of property, and consequently, no concept of theft. Possessive pronouns had little meaning for them. But they were exceptions. Generally speaking, we see theft as a bad thing. And having it prohibited as a commandment from God, not just a human law, suited the forces of law and order very well.

Do not accuse anyone falsely. This used to be construed as *always tell the truth*, even if the question was "Does my bum look big in this?" When I once found a motorcyclist on one side of a wall, his leg grotesquely broken, while the remains of his motorbike were embedded in the other side of the said wall, he asked me, "Is my bike OK?" In fact, he went on to request, "Tell me my bike's OK." So I did.

But giving false testimony doesn't mean writing *Treasure Island* when you know there's no such person as Long John Silver. And we know it. It's about basic honesty and integrity; and certainly in legal situations, the process of the law, and the freedom, even the lives of others might depend on it.

The last commandment is an odd one. *Do not covet* isn't about doing, but about being. It makes contentment, and satisfaction- states of mind, ways of being- mandatory. Covetousness might well lead to theft, but the commandment is to not be that sort of person. It doesn't prohibit ambition. Not coveting your neighbour's ass doesn't prevent you from aspiring to have one of your own. It just says that if you find your neighbour's property desirable, God is saying *don't even think about it.*

Which brings us, if you will allow the diversion, to the idea of Sin By Thought. In church, we confess that we have sinned in thought, word and deed. Sinning in deed is obvious enough, and so is sinning by word. But where does temptation become sin by thought? If I fancy another woman, and I'm tempted to do something about it, but I don't because I'm married, and I realise it would be wrong, have I resisted temptation (good), or sinned in thought (bad)? I think I know the answer. If my reasons for not committing adultery are about the likeliness of my getting caught, the effect on my marriage, and the fact that my bishop would have me out of the parish faster than Superman, I have sinned in thought. If what deters me from sexual naughtiness is the simple acknowledgement that it is wrong, because God says so, I have resisted temptation, and all I am guilty of is being a smug git.

Jesus pointed out that the Law, as written, is about behaviour, and its result. But he emphasised that there is more to it than that. We may say we haven't killed anybody. Jesus said that the sort of anger that might wish someone dead is as bad. We might say we haven't committed adultery, but Jesus' response is that lusting after another woman is as bad. The Law seems to spread its tentacles to get us. And there is the further warning that if we are guilty of breaking one commandment, we are guilty of breaking them all. The Law is not ten separate rules, but an entity. There is the powerful symbol that they are carved on stone. Breaking one would break the whole lot. And stone, famously, will not bend. We can't say we've only broken the law a bit. The whole thing seems to be contrived so that nobody could ever look at the Law and judge themselves Not Guilty.

Anyway, there is the Law. But why is the Jewish Law written up in our parish churches? If it was a code given to a particular people at one point in their history, is it really for all people at all times? This is the attitude the church has always had, because Jesus said he didn't come to abolish the law- he came to make it even more real. And that for all time, not a single dot will be removed from the Law

(Matthew 5: 17-20). Whether Jesus meant by this just the Ten Commandments, or the whole canon of the law which makes up the small print in Exodus and Leviticus is totally immaterial. Because we can't keep even the first commandment, the rest are merely Other Offences To Be Taken Into Consideration. If we haven't made God the central focus of our lives, then ploughing with an ox and a donkey yoked together is neither here nor there. Putting the Ten Commandments on the church wall represents the whole Law. But instead of being there to remind us of a guilt we ought to have, by rights, but are forgiven from, by grace, the real reason Mr Biles ornamented his tiny Dorset church with them is very different.

In the debate about capital punishment, it was often suggested that the death penalty was a deterrent. The idea of being hanged would discourage me from sticking a bread-knife into the church organist (although see above, under Sin by Thought). But others had different ideas. The prospect of punishment, they argued, was less important, as a deterrent, than the prospect of being caught. This still dominates much of our morality today. What keeps many of us from doing wrong is the likelihood of being found out, not the actual wrongness of it. But bring into the equation an all-seeing, all-knowing God, and Mr Plod now has a huge and powerful ally. I may not see you nicking the spoons, he says, *but God will*. I might not be able to punish you, *but God will*. The fear of possible detection and punishment by the state is reinforced by the fear of *certain* d and p by God. Some lurid pictures of hell over the chancel arch will help, too. With demons and fire and forks and buttocks. James Joyce, in *Portrait of the Artist of a Young Man* gives an account of a sermon on the subject of Hell delivered with an almost sadistic relish to a Catholic boys' college, that was clearly calculated to frighten its listeners into being good. I did it for O level. It worked.

For a church that courted the approval of the state, being seen to uphold the same standards of law-abiding respectability that the state itself demanded of its citizens was clearly a good move. This holds good today. Many people outside the church nevertheless look to it for moral leadership, to back up the state, and society, in condemning whatever society wants condemned. Why doesn't the church speak out against drugs, pornography, paedophilia, pub opening hours, internet chat rooms, celebrity Big Brother or whatever is exercising the tabloid press at the time? A church that proclaims sin forgiven would be seen as being just as subversive and unacceptable now as it ever was.

In March 2008, the Vatican newspaper *L'Osservatore Romano* published a new list of modern sins. The Pope deplored what he called the decreasing sense of sin in today's secularised world, (and the fact that 60% of Italian Catholics no longer go to confession) and so he defined drug abuse, genetic manipulation, causing poverty, environmental pollution and others as deadly sins. The goalposts keep moving.

But the Law, as St Paul pointed out, could never do any more than show us that we have sinned. *For no one is put right in God's sight by doing what the Law requires; what the Law does is to make man know that he has sinned* (Romans 3: 20) It could make us feel guilty, but not tell us what to do about it. Nowhere on the walls of the church does it say *Your sins are forgiven- go in peace.* That, the heart of the Gospel, the real Good News, was considered to dangerous to put in the hands of weak people like us

10 GRACE VERSUS JUSTICE

Welcome to the ringside for this heavyweight bout over fifteen rounds between, in the red corner, Justice- long standing champion, and the challenger, Grace. This isn't an easy contest to predict. Grace, a mere slip of a thing, enters the ring unarmed. Fight-fanciers are saying she's just too good to be true. Whereas Justice, although she carries a sword, has it blunted by Mercy, and she's blindfolded, too. The big money is still on Justice, though- a big girl, with good form, and very popular with the crowd. But I'm putting my stake- everything I've got, in fact- on Grace. Because I am a sinner. I won't thrill you with the details, just tell you that if Justice wins, I'm up to my neck in the good-for-the-roses. Only by Grace do I have any hope at all.

Now you know I'm biased, let's look at an action movie. It could be James Bond- plenty to choose from there- or Bruce Willis in his magic vest, anything with Steven Seagal in it, or Batman- preferably the Tim Burton ones, before they got as camp as a field full of Scouts. The action hero, human, mutant, or refugee from an exploding planet, deserves a worthy opponent, so the action movie villain must be ruthless, indifferent to the suffering of his victims, and for most of the movie, he will be On Top. At his hands (or more likely, the oversized fists of his henchmen), our Hero will take quite a pasting.

But several explosions, a couple of hours and a token love interest later, the villain will Get His. He will be thrown off something high, into something hot, shot, fed to piranhas, blown up or squashed. The climax of the action movie is the villain going "Aaargh!"

If this book was about the defeat of evil, I would point out that in James Bond movies, the evil henchmen carry on henching even when the villain is either dead, or has legged it. This means Mr Bond gets yet another action sequence under his belt, the henchman comes to a sticky end, and I would say that although the devil is comprehensively defeated by Jesus on the cross, there are still a lot of his workers active in the world who don't know the meaning of the word "beaten". But it isn't. So I won't. I will be content with Blofeld, Oddjob, Jaws (the man or the fish), the Joker, even the Alien, dying hard.

Our sense of justice is satisfied by this. We want to see the guilty punished. The mother of a child who died of e-coli poisoning from a school dinner wanted "justice for my son". She meant she wanted to see somebody punished. The parents of a child whose murder was as yet unsolved wanted justice. Somebody caught and punished.

Here in the west, it would be hard to sell a movie that had its villain repent, rather than be punished. Bollywood does it all the time. It's what Indian audiences want. But then Bollywood villains tend not to be serial killers, drug barons or potential world-dominating nutters. *The Return of the Jedi* is the only mainstream movie I can think of where the man in black, the evil Darth Vader, is redeemed. He dies anyway, mind you, so our sense of justice is served too. Sorry if you haven't seen it. I've just spoilt the ending for you. And what about him being Luke Skywalker's father, then? Surprise or what?

We also have a problem with penitence. We expect our criminals, real or fictional, to show proper contrition as they are led off to the cells. What offends us is the arrogance or self-righteousness of a criminal who shows no repentance- no sign of acknowledging that what he has done is wrong. "The prisoner showed no remorse" sometimes occurs in accounts of trials, as if to emphasise what a wicked person they were. Our sense of justice wants both penitence and punishment. (The one, you notice, doesn't get the criminal off the other. It just makes us feel better).

And this is why a gospel that says, simply, *Your sins are forgiven* is totally unacceptable to us now, just as it was to the Jews of Jesus' time. Or to an Empire struggling to keep the Pax Romana, to a medieval church in a violent world, and to anybody who feels that law and order depends on the evildoer being caught and punished.

The whole point of grace is that it is undeserved. I have been accused of preaching "cheap grace", and I have always denied it emphatically. I can't preach cheap grace. If grace isn't free, it isn't grace at all. *Chambers Dictionary* defines it as the undeserved mercy of God, and says it comes from the Latin *gratia* meaning a favour. We might say that the sinner doesn't deserve forgiveness. This is quite true. Or that the sinner has done nothing to earn forgiveness. This is also true. There is nothing we can do to earn forgiveness, and no circumstances in which we might deserve it. St Paul put it, *Sin pays its wage- death; but God's free gift is eternal life in union with Christ Jesus our Lord* (Romans 6: 23).

If I relied on God's justice, when I come to judgement, I am bang to rights, guilty as all get out, doomed. So are we all, because we are all sinners. So when people ask me why doesn't God smite sinners, I say I have no desire at all to be smitten, thank you. But if I rely on God's grace, the outlook is much brighter. Because of the death of Jesus, I have no case to answer, and I get off scot free.

And how that offends! So many people don't want to believe that, so they say it just isn't true. From feeling guilty about my sin, I now feel guilty about being let off. But not so much that I don't accept it and revel in it. At the first Sunday School I attended (Fairlop Gospel Hall- now Fairlop Evangelical Church), we sang a chorus:

God has blotted them out, I'm happy I'm glad I'm free!

God has blotted them out, I'll turn to Isaiah and see:

Chapter forty four, twenty two and three-

He's blotted them out, so now I can shout, for this- means- me!

I had to ask what he's blotted out. I was told it was my sin. This didn't stop my teachers making it clear to me, that like everyone else I was headed for hell, unless, by some slim chance, I was saved. The chap who, years later, gave out tracts outside Victoria Station, had a similar message. You are doomed, unless. It took me a while to realise that that wasn't Good News by any stretch of the imagination. The real gospel is, you are saved, because.

Not convinced yet? Let's look at Matthew 20. Here we are, quite late in Jesus' ministry. If there is a chronology in the Gospels, then it suggests that Jesus' initial teaching, *Repent, for the kingdom of Heaven is near* (Matthew 4: 17) gradually gave way to a more universal understanding of his mission in terms of geography and scope. The Syrian woman in chapter 15 taught him that he was not just for one nation and race, but for everyone, everywhere. The later parables are about grace, and forgiveness, and the unacceptability of those concepts. Make no mistake. Just as St Paul knew that the idea of grace could be misconstrued as licence, and would therefore be treated with great suspicion, so Jesus knew that he was preaching an outrageous gospel.

The story of the labourers in the vineyard shows a vine grower agreeing to pay the grape-pickers the going daily rate for a day's work. No problem. But as the day progresses, and maybe the rain-clouds gather, making the task more urgent, he takes on more workers, promising to make it right by them. And again. Finally, an hour before knocking off, he takes on the loafers and idlers, who put in a token amount of work.

When it's pay time, these are paid first- the full day's pay for an hour's work. And when those who have been up to their knuckles in grapes all day get what they had been promised- the rate for the job- they are offended, and their spokesman starts going on about differentials. *Listen, friend,* says the owner. I love that. He might have said it with an arm around his shoulder. But he might have said it with a poke in the chest. Poke someone in the chest as you call him "friend" and he will get the point. (Mind you, if you haven't got a couple of shaven-headed thugs at your shoulder, poking someone in the chest and calling him "friend" is not a good idea.) But the owner points out, it's his own money, and he can give it to whom he likes, and no, life isn't fair. Show me in the book where it says it should be.

So when you get to heaven after a lifetime of toeing the line, and apologising profusely every time your foot slipped, how will you feel about sharing it with all the rogues and rascals, rapscallions and outright crooks that God has forgiven out of sheer grace? If eating with sinners was good enough for Jesus, is it alright for you?

We only "labour" in God's vineyard in the sense that we live in this world. The actual work we do is simply the business of living. If we say that the pay packet is a reward for Good Deeds, Acts of Charity, or Not Running Off With the Gorgeous Redhead, then we do a great disservice to the whole concept of salvation by grace.

And any suggestion that I, because I'm a priest,

am working harder for God than anyone else, I reject. Remember, I'm actually paid *not* to work- my time is taken up instead by visiting sick friends, rejoicing with the lovers and the new parents, and holding the hands of the bereaved. And sharing the huge joke of sin forgiven. None of which is work. And don't give me that line about how I only work one day a week. I don't work on Sundays- I worship, and lead others in worship, and believe me, that ain't work. It's a great joy and a pleasure.

The pay packet turns out not to be a reward at all, but a free gift from a God too generous for his critics to accept. Not only had the one-hour workers been paid for doing nothing, *so had the all-day labourers*. What they received wasn't payment, but what the owner chose to give them. The fact that they'd spent the day grape-picking just meant there was a bottle of something nice to look forward to. Maybe two bottles. Who's counting?

11 PURGATORY AND THE CHANTRIES

There is a product on the market (the market being the internet, mostly), which will, it claims, give you more oxygen than you can get simply by breathing. It is taken in the form of drops diluted with water. The distributors claim that ordinary breathing can no longer give you the oxygen your body needs (this ignores the fact that there is a fair percentage of oxygen in the air you breathe out), and that taking a few drops of their product orally will increase the amount of oxygen in your bloodstream, (more nonsense, as only in the lungs do the red blood cells take on oxygen. If you could absorb gases from water, you'd fill up with carbon dioxide every time you drank fizzy water, beer, or, God forbid, Dr Pepper). And this hugely expensive product is not unique in the realm of quack medicines. The trick is first, to persuade you that you need something, whether you really do or not; second, to point out that only they can supply it; and then third, to make you pay for it. Bear this in mind as you read what follows.

Not only did the church, fairly early on, renege on its gospel of *your sins are forgiven,* it actively promoted the opposite. The doctrine of Purgatory developed very early- before the end of the second century, and is still upheld by many in the Roman

Catholic Church, and some of the Orthodox churches. It says, in effect, *Your sins are* not *forgiven*. Not all of them anyway. And as God's standard is perfection, nothing less, that leaves us still deep in the mire.

The prayer of Consecration in the service of Holy Communion in the Book of Common Prayer speaks of Jesus making *a full, perfect and sufficient sacrifice, oblation and satisfaction for the sins of the whole world*. Now despite a few technicalities, like the difference between a sacrifice and an oblation (haven't a clue- maybe try Google!), doesn't that sound to you as if the death of Jesus was sufficient for the sins of the whole world? Haven't we always preached that the death of Jesus has bought the forgiveness of all sins, big and little? Well, since you ask, no we haven't.

Just as the church adopted the Ten Commandments as its standard of morality, because it felt it needed one, and they happened to be nearest, so it decided that if it was going to be a proper religion (having put aside the notion that it might actually be the antidote to religion) it needed Rituals. Instead of telling people the gospel truth that there is absolutely nothing they had to do to secure the forgiveness of their sins except to trust God that their sins were forgiven, and then waving them goodbye at the door, the church began to teach that there was a process to go through, of contrition, confession and absolution. No animals were hurt in the making of this transaction, but a transaction it became. Later, it's true, some denominations of the church saw confession and absolution as a mutual thing- a bunch of forgiven sinners celebrating and revelling in the fact. But the mainstream churches began to see the priest as the representative of Christ on earth, and taught that he was the only one qualified to pronounce absolution. Instead of *Your sins are forgiven* being a simple statement of a pre-existent fact, it has become the end of a process. You are sorry and repentant. You confess that you have sinned- in general, along with everyone else, or in particular, privately, through the grille in the confessional booth- and the priest is then able to say, as it were, *Now your sins are forgiven*. Today, in the Church of England, only a priest may say the absolution in the form *Almighty God, who forgives all who truly repent, have mercy upon* you, *pardon and deliver* you *from all your sins*. (Common Worship version). Lay Readers, Deacons (they're the ones that wear their stoles on the slant because they're not priests yet) and anybody else, all have to say *us* and *our* instead of *you* and *your*.

So the norm became, sins were confessed, a penance was imposed, and absolution was pronounced. But those sins that were not remembered, and not confessed, and those that were committed between the last confession and death, remained, in the teaching of the church, unforgiven. And so we still need, after death, to be punished for them. And this takes place in purgatory. None of this has any basis in Scripture, but in a sort of philosophical logic.

Everyone thought theirs was the most original sin

The Orthodox churches, following the Council of Florence in 1438-9, challenged the Catholic stance on Purgatory, but to little effect. The Council of Trent, in 1545, stated:

Whereas the Catholic Church, instructed by the Holy Ghost, has from the Sacred Scriptures and the ancient tradition of the Fathers taught in Councils and very recently in this ecumenical synod that there is a purgatory, and that the souls therein are helped by the suffrages of the faithful, but principally by the acceptable Sacrifice of the Altar; the Holy Synod enjoins on the Bishops that they diligently endeavour to have the sound doctrine of the Fathers in Councils regarding purgatory everywhere taught and preached, held and believed by the faithful.

The *Catholic Encyclopaedia* says:

God requires satisfaction, and will punish sin, and this

doctrine involves as its necessary consequence a belief that the sinner failing to do penance in this life may be punished in another world, and so not be cast off eternally from God.

So forgiveness is conditional on penance, and failure to do penance in this world results in punishment in the next. Modern penances consist of the recitation of prayers, or making special devotions, so they amount to little more than a slap on the wrist. It might be a few Hail Marys, or a novena, a cycle of prayers lasting nine days. But they do have the effect of reducing prayer to a form of punishment. I once shared a room at a clergy summer school with a dog-collar much wider than my own. (Did you know that the more high church a vicar is, the wider his dog collar? Some of them look like they're wearing toilet rolls.) Anyway, this chap had spent the train journey to Winchester saying his daily prayers from his Missal, his little book, and was delighted to tell me he didn't have to pray again until Thursday evening. The sad thing is, he really meant it.

Excuse me. I feel a joke coming on. A man was making his confession. "I work in a timber-yard," he said. "And I steal stuff. The loft extension. I built it with wood I nicked. And the mother-in-law's bungalow. I stole all the wood for that, too. It's driving the truck, you see Father. It makes it so easy." "This is a serious matter," said the priest. "I want you to make a novena." "Fine," says the man. "You draw up the plans, and I'll get the wood."

So where did this doctrine of Purgatory come

from? Origen (c185- c254) stated that even those who depart this life with minor faults, are condemned to fire which burns away the lighter materials, and prepares the soul for the Kingdom of God. He based this idea on his reading of I Corinthians 3: 12-15:

Some will use gold or silver or precious metals in building on the foundation [of Jesus]; others will use wood or grass or straw. And the quality of each person's work will be seen when the Day of Christ exposes it. For on that day, fire will reveal everyone's work; the fire will test it and show its real quality. If what was built on the foundation survives the fire, the builder will receive a reward. But if anyone's work is burnt up, then he will lose it; but he himself will be saved, as if he had escaped through the fire.

But this passage, as even the *Catholic Encyclopaedia* concedes, is certainly open to different interpretation. I have never read any commentary which takes it to mean that after we are dead, we are tortured with fire until such time as God judges we have been sufficiently punished to be let into heaven.

One problem I have with the idea of Purgatory is that of Eternity. Heaven will not, I believe, be time going on and on. Death will free us from the whole business of time. There is a verse which despite John Newton not writing it, and its not fitting in, still gets shoved into *Amazing Grace: When we've been there ten thousand years, bright shining as the sun, there's no less days to sing God's praise than when we first begun.* Is it just me, or does that sound perfectly dreadful? Hard as it may be to imagine, the state of Heaven cannot, surely, be quantified in time at all. Eternity is the total absence and irrelevance of time. But those who promote the doctrine of Purgatory assert that Purgatory is for a *time-* and a very long time, too, even if our stay there can be reduced or shortened by prayers, indulgences, or masses.

St Augustine, Gregory the Great, Bede, St Bernard and others argued along the lines that Jesus would not have said there were some sinners who will not be forgiven in this world or the next (Matthew 12: 33) unless there were other sinners who, although they are not forgiven in this world, *are* forgiven in the world to come. But even this presupposes that forgiveness is through penitence and penance, rather than grace- that there is a *process* of forgiveness by which those in the world to come will be forgiven, rather than a simple pronouncement.

In 1571, under Elizabeth I, the convocation of clergy ratified the *Thirty Nine Articles of Religion,* which can still be found near the back of the Book of Common Prayer, for the partial amusement of children during sermons even more tedious than reading the 39 Articles. Article 22 states that *The Romish Doctrine concerning Purgatory, Pardons, Worshipping and Adoration, as well of Images as of Reliques, and also invocation of Saints, is a fond thing vainly invented, and grounded upon no warranty of Scripture, but rather repugnant to the Word of God.* So there. Purgatory, according to the Church of England, is "a fond thing vainly invented." Which means, (stare hard at the nearest papist here)

Someone Made It Up.

Here we need to make a diversion. Throughout this book, I have quoted the Bible, or given you the references so you can look it up for yourself. We take the Bible for granted, but its appearance in English is the result of a long and bloody struggle, itself the worthy subject of whole books.

There had been translations of the Bible into Middle English, the language of Chaucer, but the Church didn't worry too much about it, because not many people could read, so little harm was done. In 1408, the bishops of the church in England banned the translation of the Bible into English. The simplistic explanation of this action is that as long as the Church could tell you what the Bible said, and not tell you some of the things it said because it didn't want you to know (like that bit in Galatians about men and women, slaves and free, Jews and gentiles all being the same to God), then it had *power*. If you can read the Bible for yourself, and find out that the church has invented whole new sins for you to be guilty of, you might start losing respect.

The truth is a bit more complicated. Martin Luther effectively began the great movement known as the Reformation on 31st October 1517. He was professor of Biblical Studies at Wittenburg University, and wrote a paper disputing the Roman Catholic Church's stand on indulgences. More about them in a bit. Late in the previous century, the followers of John Wyclif had produced an English translation of the Bible from Jerome's Latin version (known as the Vulgate, meaning it was in the vulgar, or everyday language- Latin!) This English version wasn't actually very accurate, but Wyclif's followers believed that the Bible should be available for everyone who could read, to read.

The story of the Church's opposition to the translation of the Bible is tied up with its opposition to the Reformation. So afraid was it of the spread of Lutheran ideas that it suppressed the reading of the Bible by ordinary people. Foxe, who compiled *The Book of Martyrs,* claimed to have met a clergyman who told him, *We had better be without God's word than the Pope's.*

So. Indulgences. Originally, an indulgence was the release of a penitent sinner from a penance a priest had imposed earlier. Luther could have lived with that. But the church was teaching, and so people were believing, that an indulgence shortened the time a sinner would spend, after death, in Purgatory (see above, on time and eternity). This has not gone away. The Apostolic Penitentiary is today the Vatican body responsible for confessions and plenary indulgences.

Few Christians believed they would end up in Hell. The Catechism of the Roman Catholic Church today states that *immediately after death the souls of those who die in a state of mortal sin descend into Hell.* But the church still makes the distinction between Mortal Sin, and Venial Sin, which can be forgiven, albeit after a period in Purgatory.

The Sermon on hell gave everyone food for thought

Most western Christians before the Reformation believed they would pass through Purgatory, maybe for millions of years, before reaching Heaven, and that was a terrifying prospect- enough to make anybody afraid of death.

That purgatory was an un-Biblical doctrine; that the indulgence was an invention of the Church; that forgiveness of sins did not lie in the power of a priest, but was the free gift of a gracious God; all these could be discovered by reading the Bible. And so the church made the act of translation a heresy. William Tyndall gave us the English Bible that was the direct precursor of the King James Version. In 1536, he went to the stake for it. That needs emphasising. William Tyndall was strangled and burnt at the stake for heresy, and that heresy was to challenge, not the authority of God, but the authority of the Church, which was set on suppressing any version of the scripture that ordinary people could read, and discuss, and make up their own minds about. The Church was so protective of is power, prestige and income, which were all based on suppressing the true, liberating gospel, that it was prepared to kill. The Dan Browns of this world have not invented a church that would kill to protect itself.

Whatever the origins of the doctrine of Purgatory, the church came soon to quantify it in ways which could not possibly have any foundation in scripture, or anything else. For example, it began to teach that prayers and works of devotion from the faithful still alive in this world, can shorten a dead person's time in purgatory by a particular number of years. The concept that those who are dead are not in time at all, but in eternity, may still be there, but eternity is seen, not as the total absence of time, but its endless continuation. For example, the Castle Church in Wittenburg, where Martin Luther nailed his *95 Theses* to the door, contained relics that, if visited, would save you 1,902,202 years and 270 days of purgatorial pain. Which made it well worth the trip, yes?

Worshippers were encouraged to lessen the sentences- effectively to buy remission- of those suffering in the fires of Purgatory, by their prayers.

One of Chaucer's pilgrims telling their tales en route to Canterbury was a Pardoner. According to the church's law, a pardoner never had the right to forgive sins, or to sell indulgences. These could only be granted to people who had confessed their sins to their parish priest. Then they could buy an indulgence to relieve them of a period of punishment in Purgatory. Even at this legal level, forgiveness wasn't being proclaimed, but sold.

But there was an illegal trade, too. The building of the Vatican, as we know it today, was largely financed by the sale of indulgences. Pardoners sometimes claimed not only to be able to spare sinners from Purgatory, but from Hell itself. They sometimes went so far as to claim that if you bought an indulgence, you needn't repent, or clean up your way of life at all.

By 1212, the church realised that pardoners

were getting out of control, but repeated Papal bulls (edicts with the Pope's *bulla* or seal on them) had little effect, especially as the Church itself was making a tidy income out of Chantries. It was all very well for people to buy indulgences, or say their prayers, to spare themselves some punishment, but as the Council of Trent pointed out, in the pronouncement I quoted above, the most effective means of achieving this was through *the acceptable Sacrifice of the Altar*- in other words, the Mass. And as a lay person could not say the Mass, only a priest, it became customary for people to employ a priest to say Masses for the souls of their loved ones, or for the wealthy to make provision in their wills for Masses to be said for them. A whole class of priests grew up who were paid to say (or chant) the Masses. If any good came out of the system, it was education. These priests used their spare time, which they had quite a lot of, teaching. As far back as the Norman conquest, Chantries, as they were called, had been set up in English cathedrals and churches, but they really became numerous during the fourteenth century. The chantry chapel was originally a temporary structure, used until the required masses had sent the soul of the departed into Heaven, or until the money ran out. But many were built of elegant stone, and still cover the tombs of the great and (fairly) good in our cathedrals and large churches.

At the time of the Reformation in England, when Henry VIII began, and Edward VI in 1547 completed the suppression of the Chantries, there were 2,374 of them. The money collected, which had been paid in advance to the chantry priests, totalled more than £180,000. I have no idea what the modern equivalent of that is, but I bet it's more than a banker's bonus.

Why give away free what you can sell? In this situation, what interest did the church have in proclaiming the total, unconditional forgiveness of sins? Its interests, in the collection of revenue, the employment of priests, and the maintenance of its own influence, were served by upholding a doctrine that forgiveness could only ever be partial; that after death, nobody bar actual saints got into heaven before being taken around the corner for a good kicking; and that the church had the means to reduce the length and severity of this kicking, at a price.

There was always someone trying to beat the system

12 FOLLY TO THE WISE

Allow me to recap the argument so far. The Church has fought shy of preaching the real Gospel of sin forgiven for a number of reasons. Jesus' simple proclamation of forgiveness as a fact made the religious authority of his time see him as a threat to their business. And religion *was* a business, employing large numbers of people, and bestowing great prestige on its priesthood. The early Church dare not preach forgiveness for fear of presenting itself as being soft, and encouraging immorality, and, more to the point, illegality. In order to get in bed with the civil authorities, the church had to be seen as moral, upright, and strict.

Then the church found forgiveness was a commodity it could sell to everyone. You need forgiveness. Eternal punishment awaits you, or at best, millions of years of purgatory, but we can supply. We are the sole providers of forgiveness. And as long as the church was doing very well, thank you, purveying forgiveness to a grateful, paying clientele, the notion of forgiveness being available free, and without going through the channel of the church, was not one it wanted to promote, and did its best to suppress.

Thirdly, saying that everybody's sins are simply forgiven, before they have even been committed, so offends our sense of justice, and would make us seem weak, when what the world needs is tough talk. Straighten up and fly right.

But there is a fourth reason why the church today, just like the church in its early years, recoils from that four-word good news bulletin. St Paul recognised the problem way back then. It hasn't gone away.

I was once discussing music with a Greek girl. Honest, officer. We found we both liked Beethoven. "Which is your favourite symphony?" she asked. "The sixth," I said, because it is. She looked at me with new-found contempt. "Baby music!" she said. Her favourite was the ninth- the biggest, grandest, most complicated one. The cleverest one. The fact that I liked the one with the tunes you could whistle (The one, worst of all, that Walt Disney filled with My Little Pony centaurs) marked me out as an intellectual lightweight.

It's true. You will have noticed as soon as you picked it up that this book is not very thick. And that it has cartoons in it, which are mainly there to make it look a bit thicker than it really ought to be. There are no footnotes. No bibliography or index, so it can't be a proper theology book, can it? There is a reason for this. When I was at Theological College in Salisbury, and our unit of work for the week was given out on Thursday morning, there followed an unseemly rush to the library. The trouble was, we none of us knew what was a good book to read on any given subject. Faced with four feet of scholarship on, say, the Book of Amos, what's a chap to do?

Jim's solution was to pick a Blue book. It wasn't quite a random method, but pretty near. There was bound to be a blue book on any given subject. My way, much superior, of course, was to pick a Thin book. Given just a week to finish the task, I felt it was better to read a thin book than to skip through a thick one. There was no shortage of thick books. We all bought *On Being A Christian* by Hans Kung because it was on our lists, but hardly any of us read it, although I did look through it. There are no cartoons.

Nevertheless, we have come to associate big heavy books with serious scholarship, and maybe we think thin books are lightweight in every sense of the world. Mind you, the best book I have ever read on the important subject of God and the problem of evil is *The Third Peacock* by Robert Farrer Capon. It has 119 pages, and Jim won't have read it, because it's red.

In a world where education is considered to be of prime importance, and scholarship is respected, nobody likes to appear uneducated. So we hear people say *at this present moment in time* instead of *now, transportation* instead of *transport,* the pronouns *me* and *you* are replaced by *myself* and *yourself* regardless of context, and everyday life becomes cluttered with jargon and management-speak. Language, instead of becoming simpler, becomes ever more impenetrable. Our local infants' school put out an anti-smoking policy that covered a whole side of densely-typed A4 paper. I asked at the Governors' meeting why it didn't just say *Smoking is not allowed on any part of the school premises.* I was told that it just didn't. A policy couldn't be that simple, because, and I quote, *it would look like we hadn't really thought about it.* So a breadstick becomes an *elongated crouton for snacking purposes* and we all think how clever we are. We haven't just called it a breadstick. We've thought about it.

The Greek world, which the Romans inherited and Christianity grew up in, respected learning and wisdom above all. Probably, the most famous ancient Greeks we can think of are philosophers- Aristotle, Plato, Diogenes, Thetimes, Radiotimes and the rest. Nothing your Greeks liked better than the cut and thrust of intellectual debate. The followers of Socrates, for example, used a mixture of examination and scepticism. Study everything, they said, and be prepared to disbelieve everything. But while searching for the truth, if nothing is to be believed, truth cannot be found. Socrates, at the end of the 5th century BC had taught his followers to take nothing for granted, to question every tradition. This meant that debate could be endless. A lot of that debate would be on the nature of God, even though, or maybe because, most philosophers agreed with Socrates that God was, by his nature, unknowable. Of which more in a minute.

The whole of the Mediterranean area was, at the time the church was growing and spreading, under Roman rule. This unity of regime in the region had never happened before, and hasn't since. Yet despite this apparent Romanisation, with Roman architecture everywhere, and Roman coinage in the shops from Gibraltar to Alexandria, much of the Empire was still, effectively, Hellenic- thoroughly influence by the Greeks. This was the legacy of Alexander the Great, whose empire covered the whole eastern part of the Mediterranean- Greece itself, and modern Turkey, Syria, Israel and Egypt. Greek, not Latin, was the Roman Empire's real common language, and the Romans respected not only the old Greek religion (re-naming their gods and goddesses, but telling the same stories about them), but its culture and philosophy as well. And St Paul was very much aware that the gospel- *your sins are forgiven*- would be unacceptable to a lot of these Hellenised people, because it was just too simple:

For God in his wisdom made it impossible for people to know him by means of their own wisdom. Instead, by means of the so-called "foolish" message we preach, God decided to save those who believe. Jews want miracles for proof, and Greeks look for wisdom. As for us, we proclaim the crucified Christ, a message that is offensive to the Jews, and nonsense to the Gentiles...For what seems to be God's foolishness is wiser than human wisdom...(I Corinthians 1: 21- 25)

What would Greeks, used to the philosophies of the giants in their field, who would sit in the porch (if they were Stoics) discussing great ideas, like the nature of truth itself, make of a gospel that could be expressed in four words? It would have seemed mere foolishness, a faith fit only for children. Paul could imagine learned, serious Greeks listening, and asking *is that it?*

And so, almost inevitably, the church sought to intellectualise its gospel, to make it worthy of serious philosophical study. As intelligent people turned away in disappointment, the call followed them- *Wait- there's more! It isn't as simple as that!* Christian theology was born.

And almost immediately, Christian theology begat Gnosticism. From the Greek *gnosis* meaning knowledge. Gnosticism was a whole series of belief systems which claimed to receive special knowledge about God from God himself, and it was having this knowledge that secured salvation. Gnosticism was popular in Egypt, where it followed an older tradition of salvation through knowledge. In ancient Egyptian belief, the passage of a soul through the underworld to the blessings of the afterlife meant knowing the correct answers to an almost interminable series of questions, which assorted demons and demigods would ask on the way. Although the ancient Egyptian was allowed to cheat, having a copy of *The Book of the Dead* buried with him, with all the answers in. which was, in effect, a crib.

The roots of Gnosticism are there in the Old Testament, at least after the translation into Greek. This Greek Old Testament, known as the Septuagint, because seventy scholars put their heads together to produce it, was influenced by Greek ways of thinking. Actually, I stand corrected there. A Jewish friend tells me that a) there were seventy two of them. b) They worked independently, and all their translations turned out to be identical, and c) this was considered proof enough that what they had produced was what God wanted. But no matter. The Law becomes associated with wisdom, and wisdom with enlightenment. (In the book of Proverbs, Wisdom is personified as a female, and she is described as worth pursuing, wooing, and winning.) The opposites- evil and folly, become symbolised by darkness. The Jewish monks who lived at Qumran, by the Dead Sea, left the Dead Sea Scrolls, hidden in jars in caves. They contain the Old Testament (except the Book of Esther, which was on loan to the besieged Jews at Masada, who never had the chance to give it back); the community's rule of life, and the descriptions of the war between the Children of Light and the Children of Darkness. This was how they saw their world- the physical world reflected the conflict that went on, and would go on, at a cosmic level. The New Testament many times uses the images of light and darkness to represent good and evil, the saved and the lost. But in Greek Christian communities, the old association of enlightenment and knowledge encouraged the idea that we are saved, not by our faith, or even by our deeds, but by our knowledge. This certainly appealed to the intellectuals. The idea of having secret knowledge, passed on only to initiates, the shared notion that only *we* know the truth about God, gave Christianity a cachet that cults like Kabbalah and Scientology have today. Even Freemasonry owes some of its appeal to the idea that sharing knowledge makes us a group apart. We know something you don't know. And when it becomes a matter of eternal life, or eternal damnation, as the Gnostic Christians would have it, then that knowledge, or the lack of it, was seen to be crucial. Anybody in this atmosphere who tries to say the gospel, and the whole of the gospel, is *Your sins are forgiven* will be considered childish. Whole books have been written about Gnosticism. Some of them are quite thick.

St Paul tried to turn the idea of Gnosticism on its head. It isn't about us knowing about God, he says, but God in his grace acknowledging us. There is evidence that some of the ideas in his letters are his deliberate counter to Gnostic ideas. In I Corinthians 8: 1-3, he says, *it is true, of course, that "all of us have knowledge" as they say. Such knowledge, however, puffs a person up with pride; but love builds up. Whoever thinks he knows something really doesn't know as he ought to know. But the person who loves God is known by him.*

The apostle John also seems to have known about Gnosticism, and would have none of it. In the beginning of his first letter, emphasises that he speaks of what he knows from real experience, not what he has deduced philosophically. But then he announces *God is light, and there is no darkness at all in him* (I John 1: 5). John is speaking the language of Gnosticism, or of the Essene Jews of Qumran. Very soon, Christians began addressing their opponents in their opponents' own language. This began the process of intellectualising Christianity, smothering its simple, liberating gospel under jargon.

The Unknowability of God

Sorry, that was more than a moment. The Unknowablilty of God ought to be a given, yet the trouble with theology is that very few people are prepared to admit that nobody knows anything about God. Not really. By faith, we can believe what God has revealed about himself in the Bible. By faith we can believe that Jesus is God revealing himself to us in human form. But that's about it. If somebody asks me, *How do you know God exists?* I have to reply, *I don't. But I* believe *God exists.* The Greeks would have been content to make this alone the subject of debate worthy of their intellect.

All those books on theology are not really the study of God himself. How could they be? They are about what other people have thought and theorised. The objective Truth about God is not accessible. Whatever we say must necessarily be speculation. From the Christian point of view, it is informed speculation, since we have the Bible. But that's about it.

Just once, St Paul was tempted to join in the intellectual debate. In Athens, some Epicurean and Stoic teachers debated with him (Acts 17: 16-34). Epicureans taught that the pursuit of happiness is mankind's true vocation. The Stoics' basic philosophy was Life Is A Sod. Get On With It. Both these types, disagreeing with each other, at least agreed about Paul. They referred to him as ignorant. (As Eugene Petersen, in his translation *The Message* puts it, *What an airhead!* which is quite clear). But when Paul saw that they had covered all their exits pretty thoroughly, to the extent of raising an altar to an Unknown God, he latched onto this, and proclaimed Jesus as that unknown God. Some people made fun of him when he spoke of the resurrection, and Luke tells us that a man named Dionysius, and a woman named Damaris believed him, and some other people. That was it. There was no mass conversion here. There is no Letter of Paul to the Athenians. His simple gospel wasn't acceptable to clever, intellectual Greeks. No matter. It was after this that Paul vowed to preach nothing by Christ crucified. But whereas Paul eschewed the intellectual in favour of the simple and unadorned gospel, the rest of the church joined in the intellectual debate with gusto. We might remember that Jesus said *I assure you that whoever does not receive the Kingdom of God like a child will never enter it* (Mark 10: 15). But mostly we don't.

One of the joys of worshipping with the Greek Orthodox Church is seeing babies in arms having warmed wine spooned into them at the Eucharist. At Baptism, they are members of the Church, and share in all the privileges that brings. Not so in the Church of England. We baptise babies, sure. But we don't admit people to share the bread and wine of Holy Communion until they have been Confirmed- the Bishop lays hands on them, with the words, "Receive the Holy Spirit." And Confirmation happens, at the earliest, in the teens, after a course of instruction. In the Scriptures, the Creeds, the Commandments, on the traditions of the church and its worship, on the meaning of the Eucharist itself. The Bishop will not confirm a person who has not been suitably prepared.

True, the Church will confirm those who don't have the intellectual capacity to receive instruction, but who show they love the Lord. But by and large, the notion of accepting the Kingdom of God like a child is lost under our condition that admission to the full, participating membership of the church is a matter of understanding, and knowledge.

This carries on into our worship and liturgy as well. Services in church are sometimes padded out, as if length added to dignity. And take the Blessing at the end of the service. All that is needed is something on the lines of *The peace of God, and his blessing be with you.* This, by the way, is another example of what only a priest can do. A lay person would have to say *with us,* because they can't really bless in the name of God, only ask him nicely if he will bless us.

But we want a proper blessing, so we have *The peace of God, which passes all understanding, keep your hearts and minds in the knowledge and love of God, and of his Son, Jesus Christ our Lord. And the blessing of God, Father, Son and Holy Spirit, be with you evermore.* There. That's a proper blessing! Or is it? A lot of clergy now insert ...*and all those dear to you* before that *evermore.* And Canon Roger Royle, concluding *Sunday Half Hour* on Radio 4, used to add *in this world and the next* as well. You see? Why use a few words when a lot would do? Because we want to cross all our theological eyes, and dot all our tees, the Eucharistic

Prayers, from the Book of Common Prayer onward, have become hugely wordy. And where there is a choice of prayers, as in *Common Worship,* there is actual resistance to the shortest one, simply because it's short. And look at the prayers of thanksgiving after the Holy Communion. A page each. We can't just say *Thank you,* can we?

So there is our fourth reason for keeping the simple Gospel to ourselves. It's not big, and it's not clever.

13 WORK

Jesus said, *I assure you that whoever does not receive the Kingdom of God like a child will never enter it* (Mark 10: 15- in Matthew and Luke as well). Children are very good at receiving things, and adults often aren't. They do not look for the catch, or question whether it is real. I have a very funny book called *Great lies to tell small kids*. My favourite is that if you put a slice of ham in a DVD player, it will show a film about pigs. Children believe stuff. I once managed to convince my boys for a whole afternoon that the whole world used to be in black and white, and we didn't have colour at all until 1967, and showed them the black and white photographs as evidence. Jesus meant that the Kingdom is to be accepted the way children accept. There is no cost. There is no catch. Just accept it. This doesn't mean that we leave our brains behind when we consider our faith. We are still told to love God with all our minds. But it doesn't detract from the fact that God's forgiveness is ours, without our deserving, earning, or even asking for it.

And this brings me to my final argument. The church has been so reluctant to preach those four little words because, quite frankly, we don't want to hear them. I have spoken about *the church* throughout this book as shorthand when I have really meant the churches' leadership and hierarchy. The bums on the pews have just accepted what they were told. The churches' power in the Middle Ages depended on it. But in this case, I suspect the church knew its rank and file membership pretty well, and like the man who legendarily stood in central London trying, and mostly failing, to give five pound notes away to passers-by, knew that generally speaking, it would have very little take-up.

What it all comes down to is this. A lady on the radio just this morning was explaining her formula for a long and happy marriage. "You don't get anything in this world without hard work," she said, "and you have to work hard at your marriage." It was the first bit that got me. The assumption that you don't get anything in this world without hard work.

In the Manchester City Art Gallery hangs the great painting by Ford Madox Brown, *Work.* It took him eleven years to paint, starting in 1852, and it shows part of the road in Hampstead being dug up by noble workmen with shovels- the prototypes of much Soviet art showing square-jawed, muscular heroes. They are surrounded by others who are either watching or not; involved or simply passing by. It is a very Victorian picture, and I first met it in a 1932 booklet, *Towards the Light,* published under the name of Joseph Bibby, the animal feed and soap manufacturer, who published an annual between 1906 and 1922 extolling his religious, philanthropic and socialist principles. Here in the centre page spread, the painting is reproduced in colour, surrounded by the following improving texts. (The references aren't there- I had to look them up):

Seest thou a man diligent in his business? He shall stand before kings (Proverbs 22: 29). *Neither did we eat any man's bread for naught; but wrought with labour and travail night and day* (2 Thessalonians 3: 8).

I must work while it is day, for the night cometh when no man can work (John 9: 4).

I guess you get the idea. But Joseph Bibby, or rather, his editor, has also added a commentary on the painting, which begins: *Two important thoughts are suggested by this picture: (1) The nobility of work, and (2) the variety of work that has to be done. There is no nobility in the idler; he loses the dignity and independence that belong only to the industrious; ceasing to rely on his own exertions, he leans upon others, with the consequent deterioration of both mind and body.* He goes on to praise the honest workmen, to include "thinkers" among their ranks, and to contrast them with the idle rich and the idle poor- examples of both of which are found in Ford Madox Brown's painting.

Here is a good example of the Work Ethic- the belief that has come down through history that Work is Good, and Idleness is Bad. In fact, the whole thing is justified by the text beneath the reproduction of *Work: In the sweat of thy face shalt thou eat bread* (Genesis 3: 19). Man works because God decreed it. In the Garden of Eden, man could just swan about, giving animals silly names like *potto* and *aye-aye, and* picking fruit from the trees, (with one important reservation, mind), but in the real world, expelled from the Garden, he has to work. When the first Europeans visited the islands of Polynesia in the early eighteenth century, they found whole populations living in what they could only describe as idleness. There was fruit on the trees, fish in the sea, a climate that made house building or even dressing largely unnecessary, and it annoyed the hell out of them. It was disgraceful. These people were shamelessly immodest, had no sense of property (the concept of theft had largely passed them by), but worst of all, they were *idle*. Even in the 1950s, when Thor Heyerdahl's expedition moved on from Easter Island to Rapaiti, to explore its hilltop fortresses, they found it impossible to persuade the native men to work. There was nothing they needed that the archaeologists could offer. Only the women would work, because they were paid in dress-material.

Whereas simpler societies see work as something which must be done in order to get what they want, modern Western society has come to see work as the reason for our being, and a person's job as what defines them. At parties, the first thing we tend to ask people isn't "Do you like the Byrds?" or "Do you like Chinese food?" but "What do you do?" even though the first two are far more important if I want to see you again. And asking people what they do isn't always a good idea. I once asked a girl what she did, and she said she was an analyst in a hospital. "What do you analyse?" I asked. "On a good day," she said, "blood."

We have come to admire the self-made millionaire, who has made his fortune through his hard work. We might envy the lottery winners, but there is nothing to admire them for. We still respect hard work. Some people find even a little idleness a cause for guilt. One of my sons- the nurse- has an enormous capacity for lying beside a pool on holiday, reading a book. And not literature, either. Just a book. I envy him. Even on holiday, I like to walk, to swim, to feel I've earned my beer. People newly retired find the lack of work difficult to come to terms with. They often have the feeling they ought to be Doing Something. And many at work find themselves pressured into working longer and longer hours. This is true: a friend who works in computers was applying for a job in New York, preparing a large company's computers for the year 2000, when all computers were expected to crash, as were the planes they were keeping airborne. They were impressed with his CV and his abilities, and they told him about the facilities they had to offer. "The staff restaurant is open 24/7," he was told. "You want a steak and fries at four in the morning, you just ask." My friend pointed out that as far as he was concerned, there was no such thing as four in the morning- not at work, anyway. He didn't get the job.

The Work Ethic is often referred to as the Protestant Work Ethic, because its appreciation in Christian terms grew out of the teachings of Luther and Calvin. Luther taught that work is man's duty in the world. He works, not just for himself, but for the benefit of society. But Luther also embraced the doctrine of Predestination. This can be argued like this. Some people will be saved, and some will be damned. God knows everything, so he knows (and has known since before creation) who is who. As God knows who will be saved and who not, and does nothing to change the situation, it is his will. Somehow, the elect atheist will be brought to faith and salvation. One destined to be damned can do nothing about it. And John Calvin, one of Luther's followers, believed and taught that although we cannot know who is saved and who will end up on the sharp end of a toasting fork, the fact that a person works diligently is a good indication that he is one of the elect, and the idler is sending out pretty good clues that he isn't. Work is a sign that we recognise God's grace working in us. Labour is a sign of salvation.

Every vicar has vagrants turning up at the Vicarage sometime or other. We give them food and hot drinks, the chance to warm up, an opportunity to talk if they want to. One I remember would accept nothing from us- not even a mug of tea- unless he worked first. He would weed the churchyard path, or trim the hedge. He wouldn't wash the car. "I don't do water," he explained. But here was a man at the very lowest level of society, too proud to accept anything for nothing.

Going back to that commentary on the painting, independence is seen to be a great virtue. The worker is self-reliant. Self-reliance is good. Leaning on others, being dependent, leads not only to a lack of respect from others, but to a correct lack of self-respect. And yet Christianity should be about our reliance, not on our own merits, abilities or works, but on God's grace. *We do not presume to come to this thy table, merciful Lord, trusting in our own righteousness, but in thy manifold and great mercies,* as the prayer of humble access in the Communion service has it.

The whole notion of leaning entirely on God, trusting him in all things, is at the heart of our faith. The work ethic has come full circle. A doctrine of work that was informed by a particular interpretation of Christian faith, has been read back into our faith, to the extent that now, the simplicity of the message is obscured by the doctrine of work.

A favourite text of those who believe that our salvation depends on our own efforts is Philippians 2: 12, where Paul exhorts his readers to *keep on working with fear and trembling to complete your salvation.*

Salvation is, according to much of the church's teaching, something that has to be worked at. As I pointed out, we respect the millionaire who has worked for his money, not the lottery winner who has just got lucky. We respect the Christian who has worked tirelessly for he church, given herself in the service of others for Jesus' sake, or even gone the way of ceaseless prayer in the coarse habit of asceticism. To the extent that anyone who preaches *your sins are forgiven* to the prostitute and the tax-collector (make that the drug dealer, just for good measure- both prey on their fellow citizens for profit) is preaching an outrageous, unacceptable gospel.

Nothing worthwhile comes easily, we are told.

What we work hard and save for, we appreciate the more. If a thing costs nothing, we tend to regard it as worth nothing. And as nobody is going to say salvation isn't worth having, nobody suggests that forgiveness of sins isn't what we all need, it must, therefore, be difficult to obtain. Time and again, we are told that the Christian life is a difficult one. Jesus foretold that his followers would suffer hardships and persecutions, and in some parts of the world, they still do. But in the western world today, that is hardly the case. The worst most of us might have to face is ribbing from colleagues at work. Yes, there will be hardships in most of our lives. For example, few people will never experience bereavement. But that's life.

Even those who accept that our salvation is through faith alone, and not through works, often somehow manage to turn faith into just a different sort of work- believing lists of stuff, rather than its proper meaning of *trust*- we are saved just by accepting that we are saved, forgiven by accepting that we are forgiven.

People today don't want to hear this. It is too easy to value things according to what they cost. Whole industries are based on it. Even beer is advertised as being "reassuringly expensive"- it *must* be good if it costs that much. And those CDs and DVDs that were given away free with the newspapers too often ended up scaring the birds off the vegetable patch. If the church has treated forgiveness as a product it can sell, it might be because it found it couldn't give it away anyway. The ethic of work is deeply embedded, as is the suspicion of anything that can be obtained without it. The grace of God is still outrageous.

14 THE CHURCH TODAY

Once upon a time there was a country church, supported, broadly, by three families. Two were the churchwardens, and the third were weekenders with enough clout to insist on the Book of Common Prayer and the King James Version of the Bible, or they wouldn't come. They rewarded this by putting a £50 note in the collection plate. Then the benefice (the parish shared its Vicar with a neighbouring village) gained a curate, of the Female Persuasion, and the little parish noticed with alarm that when she came to lead worship, the weekender either didn't come into the church after looking in at the door, or if he was already there, led his family out- taking, of course, his £50 note with him. The churchwardens asked the Vicar not to have the curate (who, personally, they claimed to both like and respect) lead their worship, because they needed the money. Their temptation to say *tough- if they won't accept her ministry, stuff them-* was overcome by the fond remembrance of the big one in the collection. They were saying, in effect, that they wanted this man and his family to come to church because they wanted his money. And they were prepared to do almost anything to keep him.

Part of the condition for the Church of England ordaining women to the priesthood was the establishment of Alternative Episcopal Oversight- the so-called "Flying Bishops" to provide for those who in all conscience couldn't accept that decision, but who wanted to stay in the Church of England. This is by way of introducing the Bishop of Ebbsfleet, whose "diocese" is scattered amongst other, geographical, dioceses rather like yeast in dough, seed sown in a field, however you want to figure it. He is one of a number of Bishops to those who won't accept as their Bishop anyone who has sullied his hands ordaining women. Anyway, in a letter to the *Church Times,* in February 2008, the then Bishop shared the Ebbsfleet Rule of Life:

It is intended, *he wrote,* to suggest positive engagement with the Christian life, and has been welcomed by those of other traditions. Its seven clauses hint at the search for perfection to which the Lord calls us, however much we fall short:

1. We attend the Eucharist and receive Holy Communion, especially on Sundays and principal feasts and holy days.

2. We study Holy Scripture regularly, especially the Gospel of the Day.

3. We take some part in Daily Prayer, whether at church or at home.

4. We practise examination of life and habits of quietness and solitude.

5. *We give generously and regularly to support the work of the Church.*

6. *We give of our talents and time in the service of others, mindful of our responsibilities as citizens.*

7. *We pray and work for justice and peace and the coming of God's kingdom.*

What struck me about that was items 5 and 6. Notice that our *giving-* that is, our money, is given to the work of the church. Our *time and talents* are offered to the community, as citizens. And church attendance is top of the list, above Bible study and prayer.

One Sunday in early September, just after the children have gone back to school, the Church of England designates as Back to Church Sunday. Egged on by the diocese, supplied with leaflets and posters, and for some reason, balloons, we are to encourage our congregations to bring with them to church a friend, a neighbour, maybe someone who used to go to church but stopped. It seems to make little difference, but the church feels it must do something to get more bums on pews.

Because? We might say that we want to get people into church so we can share the Good News of Jesus' love, of sins forgiven, death conquered. In some churches, that may well be the case. I once asked the congregation of my rural parish why we wanted more people to come to church. One elderly man said, *because it's more fun when there's a lot of us here. The singing's better.* But he was alone. Everybody else agreed we wanted more people to come because we needed their money.

The story goes that a passenger jet was in a terminal dive. The cabin crew asked, "Is anyone here religious?" A Christian raised his hand. "Do something!" pleaded the stewardess. So he took a collection. The church and its ever-outstretched hand are inseparable in public perception, but whereas the church in the New Testament and its formative years collected money for the relief of the poor, to feed the hungry, to aid widows and orphans when there was no welfare state, the church today mostly raises funds for itself. Instead of being the source and channel of charity, it has become a charity itself.

For most parish churches, the biggest call for money comes from the Diocese. Apart from the stipend, pension and housing costs for the clergy, the diocese has the Bishops, with their houses, offices and expenses, the cathedral and its staff, Church House (the diocesan office) with its own staff, and also a whole network of education officers, Mission, Evangelism and Parish Development officers, social responsibility, ministerial training and administration officers. The cost of all this falls on the parishes. The Diocese of Bath and Wells in the year 2016, had a budget of £11,700,000. Of this, £9,600,000 came from the parishes, in the form of the "Parish Share".

Most church buildings are listed, grade II, which means that, apart from the planning restrictions that implies, the owners, that is the churchwardens and the church council, are not able to simply let them go. If a building has outlived its usefulness, or if the cost of its repair and maintenance has gone beyond what the parish can afford, there is no escape. It cannot be allowed simply to decay. Money must be raised to maintain it. By the way, if a church is actually declared redundant, the cost of maintaining it is transferred to the Church Commissioners. This only spreads the cost through the church as a whole, and reduces the amount the church has for other purposes. But oddly, a redundant church is often kept in far better condition than a working one. In Essex, the parish churches of Fingringhoe Doe and Fingringhoe Wick share a churchyard- they are only a few yards apart. Some years ago, one was, sensibly, made redundant, and stood unused in excellent condition, while the parish struggled to maintain the other, which they actually worshipped in.

Churchgoers are enjoined to give. Some churches encourage them to tithe- that is, to give a tenth of their income, like the Jews of Jesus' time. Some church members actually do this. But the church too often equates giving to God with giving to the Church, and so diverts charitable giving from helping the poor, the hungry and the genuinely needy, into its own bureaucracy.

If you are a member of a parish church, then most of this chapter will be all too familiar to you. If you are a member of a Parochial Church Council (PCC) then it will probably reinforce your feelings of hopelessness and despair, without the crumb of comfort that knowing others are worse off than you is meant to bring. Sorry about that.

The Parish Share is by far the biggest expense any parish has to meet. Paying the parish clergy is the largest part, and housing those clergy who are full time, or are "house for duty", which means they perform their work of ministry in exchange for being housed. Then there is a contribution to the cost of the national church, which includes the cost of training clergy. Thirdly, there is *the cost of running the services which the diocese provides; some of these are statutory, others are in accordance with the diocesan policy, set by the Bishop, his Council and the Synod.*

My own last parish, for example, was in rural Surrey. I suppose it is fairly typical. For the year 2008, the ministry payment was £40,300. The other shared costs were £28,815. So the parish has to find, to pay the diocese, £69,115. This was a parish with four churches, and Sunday congregations totalling about 80. The parish had an adult population of 1,764, and 186 members on its Electoral Roll- those who were registered as church members, and could vote at its annual meeting. This means that every member needed to contribute £371.59 just for the diocese- just over £7.00 a week.

Four village churches. Why not do without a couple? W. H. Smith wouldn't have four branches in one town, would he? The trouble is, as I said earlier, all the buildings are Grade II historic buildings. This means we can't just abandon them. We have the responsibility under law to maintain them in good repair. So they had, as well as the diocesan share, to pay for heating and lighting, maintenance and repair, so the total annual expenditure was over £107,000. Or £11.00 per person, per week.

Faced with costs like this, year on year and rising way faster than the rate of inflation, it is hardly surprising that most of the activity of most parish churches focuses on fundraising. Appeals for what is usually known as "outward giving"- the church's contribution to charities like Christian Aid, the Children's society, or topical disaster funds, famine relief and medical charities, are often difficult to introduce. Charity begins at home. We need this money for ourselves. So much of the energy of the church is directed inward. When I tried to introduce a more regular pattern of outward giving, I was told that people would simply not give, if they thought their contribution was going to lepers, or the blind, rather than the upkeep of their village church building. A churchwarden in a previous parish longed for me to get my evangelical ambitions under control, "so we can get back to our real business-fundraising!" Jumble sales, flower festivals, concerts, fetes and bazaars are all regular ways of raising funds. True, they may well be enjoyable. True, they bring in very little compared with the sums needed. So every now and then, parishes will embark on a Stewardship Campaign. This is usually accompanied by a disclaimer on the lines that *it's not just about the money- it's about our time and talents as well.* Ignore that. It's about the money.

Guildford Diocese has established a network of Parish Stewardship Promoters- in other words, it has asked each parish to appoint somebody to *promote the clear message that Christian Stewardship is an inseparable part of our Christian journey and discipleship, and that it has a proper place in the principles we apply in handling our money and using our time. How we use money is a matter which God is concerned with* (Bishop of Guildford, February 2008).

In other words, the diocese, aware that most parishes cannot easily raise the money they demand from them, will make someone in each parish responsible, and maybe through training, better able to raise the funds.

At parish level, the Church of England is concerned with fund raising, for its own building, and to support a diocesan machinery it didn't ask for, doesn't feel it needs, and rarely calls upon. Fundraising for outside charities is necessarily secondary. Parishioners are encouraged to give *to the church*. In an ideal situation, to tithe their income *to the church*.

Mission is usually seen, not in terms of taking a simple gospel of God's love and forgiveness out into the world, but as bringing people into the church. We see our success in terms of numbers of people attending. And not because we now have the chance to tell them, week on week, "Your sins are forgiven" (How many times do you need to hear that before you believe it?) but because they will put their money in the plate, or if we're really lucky, make a standing order from their bank account. And in some dioceses, get this; the number of people attending is used to calculate the share the parish church pays. So their "success" in bringing more people in is rewarded by the demand for even more money.

So the Gospel of grace and forgiveness is not one that a lot of today's churches want to share. If God will love us, forgive us and accept us whether we go to church or not, we might not go, right? The writer of the letter to the Hebrews said, "Let us not give up the habit of meeting together, as some are doing. Instead, let us encourage one another all the more…" (Hebrews 10: 25, Good News Bible) And do you know, that's still the only verse I can find in the whole Bible that says anything about going to church being a good idea?

So the church in the past has had all sorts of reasons for suppressing the simple, joyful Gospel-Your Sins Are Forgiven. To keep in with the authorities, to be respectable, and now, simply to keep the roof on the building.

Go to church. Spend time conscious of God's presence. Enjoy his company and the company of other Christians. Have a good sing. But don't ever feel that your salvation depends on it, or that skipping church is a sin. And even if it was, it would be forgiven. That's grace. Outrageous Grace.